MAX notes®

Sandra Cisneros'

The House on Mango Street

Text by
Elizabeth L. Chesla
(M.A., Columbia University)
Department of Social Sciences
Polytechnic University
Brooklyn, NY

Illustrations by
Karen Pica

Research & Education Association
Visit our website at
www.rea.com

Research & Education Association
61 Ethel Road West
Piscataway, New Jersey 08854
E-mail: info@rea.com

MAXnotes® for
THE HOUSE ON MANGO STREET

Published 2012

Printed in the United States of America

Library of Congress Control Number 2005902189

ISBN-13: 978-0-87891-020-5
ISBN-10: 0-87891-020-4

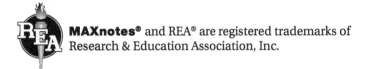

What **MAXnotes** *Will Do for You*

This book is intended to help you absorb the essential contents and features of Sandra Cisneros' *The House on Mango Street* and to help you gain a thorough understanding of the work. The book has been designed to do this more quickly and effectively than any other study guide.

For best results, this **MAXnotes** book should be used as a companion to the actual work, not instead of it. The interaction between the two will greatly benefit you.

To help you in your studies, this book presents the most up-to-date interpretations of every section of the actual work, followed by questions and fully explained answers that will enable you to analyze the material critically. The questions also will help you to test your understanding of the work and will prepare you for discussions and exams.

Meaningful illustrations are included to further enhance your understanding and enjoyment of the literary work. The illustrations are designed to place you into the mood and spirit of the work's settings.

The **MAXnotes** also include summaries, character lists, explanations of plot, and part-by-part analyses. A biography of the author and discussion of the work's historical context will help you put this literary piece into the proper perspective of what is taking place.

The use of this study guide will save you the hours of preparation time that would ordinarily be required to arrive at a complete grasp of this work of literature. You will be well prepared for classroom discussions, homework, and exams. The guidelines that are included for writing papers and reports on various topics will prepare you for any added work which may be assigned.

The **MAXnotes** will take your grades "to the max."

Larry B. Kling
Chief Editor

Contents

**Each part includes List of Characters,
Summary, Analysis, Study Questions and
Answers, and Suggested Essay Topics.**

SECTION ONE

Introduction

The Life and Work of Sandra Cisneros

"If I were asked what it is I write about," says Sandra Cisneros, "I would have to say I write about those ghosts inside that haunt me." These ghosts—of poverty, sexism, and racism—populate *The House on Mango Street*, the novel that won Cisneros the Before Columbus American Book Award in 1985 and also won the hearts of thousands of readers across America. Originally published in 1984, this brilliant collage of character sketches and stories is revolutionary in its simple, honest look at issues such as the discrimination, poverty, and domestic violence faced by Mexican-American women.

What is so enchanting about Cisneros' novel, for both young and adult readers, is not only its patchwork-quilt structure, the honesty of the narrator's voice, or the beauty and simplicity of the language. Rather, the triumph of *Mango Street* is the way it empowers its readers. Full of characters who lack power—socially, politically, economically, and sexually—the novel is not a story of despair, but of hope, which is what the narrator's name, Esperanza, means in English.

Cisneros, who was born in Chicago in 1954, is the only daughter in a family of six sons. Though she spent her childhood cramped in apartments much too small for her large family, she often felt alone. Her brothers "paired themselves off," she says, thus leaving her "the odd-woman-out forever." In addition, the Cisneros family moved around a great deal, shuttling back and forth between Chicago and Mexico City, where her father's family lived. Cisneros was never in one place long enough to develop true friendships with other children her age.

Cisneros found refuge from her loneliness in reading. Books became her best friend, and she buried herself in them. It was not long before Cisneros began to compose stories in her head, forming narratives out of the daily events of her life. Fortunately for Cisneros, her mother, a Chicana (Mexican-American), supported her desire to read. To give her daughter the opportunities she herself was denied, Cisneros' mother freed her from the traditional domestic duties of a Chicana female. She excused Cisneros from cooking, cleaning, and babysitting so Cisneros could study and read.

Growing up in a family full of men and in the *barrios,* Cisneros was well aware of the patriarchal structure of the Chicano society, which denied women equality at every level. As a teen she determined to fight this *machismo* (the Latin American term for male chauvinism) and to move from the ranks of the powerless to the powerful. Certainly her mother's emphasis on education helped Cisneros in this quest. But it was through writing that she felt most able to help herself and other women.

In grade school Cisneros began recording her stories in a spiral notebook that she never showed to anyone. In high school, however, she was known among her classmates as a poet and was the editor of her school's literary magazine. In her junior year at Loyola University of Chicago, where she received a B.A. in English, she took her first creative writing class.

It wasn't until Cisneros attended the Writers Workshop in Iowa, however, that she found her true voice as a writer. There, she says, "for the first time in my life I felt 'other'." After thinking about what it was that made her different from her classmates, she realized that her impoverished childhood and the characters that populated her past were worthy of writing about because they were different from the mainstream, different from the "norm" that radiated from television sets across the nation.

After Iowa, Cisneros returned to the *barrios* to teach high-school dropouts. This didn't leave her much time for writing, however, so she quit and took a job at Loyola, where she recruited and counseled minority and disadvantaged students. Both of these experiences were important in her development as a Chicana feminist and writer. The stories she heard from these students from the *barrios* were much like her own, and she realized there was a vast population of "the powerless" that she needed to address and whose stories needed to be told.

Cisneros began to incorporate these stories into the project she'd been working on since Iowa. The result was *The House on Mango Street*, a story whose protagonist discovers that power and peace come from recognizing one's place in and one's duty to the community.

Today, Cisneros is also the author of *Woman Hollering Creek*, a collection of short stories, and *My Wicked Wicked Ways*, a collection of poems. She has been awarded two NEA Fellowships for writing and a Dobie-Paisano Fellowship. Although she has not stopped writing, she has been teaching for the past several years as a guest writer at universities across the country.

Historical Background

It is no wonder that Cisneros, a woman of Mexican-American heritage, is obsessed with writing about the powerless. The history of Mexican-Americans is filled with conquests and inequalities—as is the history of women.

Although the Spanish were first to "conquer" the so-called "New World," it was not long before those who had settled on the land found themselves in turn being conquered. In 1848, at the close of the Mexican-American War, the United States and Mexico signed the infamous Treaty of Guadalupe Hidalgo, which gave approximately 50 percent of Mexico's territory—what is now Texas, New Mexico, California, Arizona, Nevada, Utah, and half of Colorado—to the United States. In 1906, Mexico plunged into a depression, sending a wave of new immigrants over the border. This wave was soon followed by another, in 1910, when revolutionary forces began a ten-year civil struggle in Mexico. In fact, according to historian Earl Shorris, between 1880 and 1929 alone more than a million Mexican immigrants came to the United States.

But the country they came to did not always welcome them with open arms. Instead, many immigrants faced flagrant discrimination and were often denied their basic civil and human rights.

Mexican and Mexican-American laborers were frequently exploited for cheap labor, especially on farms in California and elsewhere in the Southwest. In the 1930s, when the United States faced a depression of its own and jobs were scarce, Americans demanded that these immigrants be repatriated—that is, sent back to Mexico. Despite the clear violation of civil liberties, government agencies deported approximately half a million Mexican-Americans during this decade.

In the 1940s through the 1960s—especially during World War II, the Korean War, and the Vietnam War—the United States and Mexican governments set up programs that allowed *braceros*, or hired hands, temporary employment in the United States. The *braceros* came to take the place of American men at war. But United States employers often violated the terms of these agreements and denied the *braceros* such basic rights as decent food and housing.

There were also those Mexicans called *mojados*, or wetbacks—illegal workers who swam across the river between Mexico and the United States in search of jobs and a better life. These illegal immigrants were also often exploited, despite such governmental policies as the Fair Employment Practices Committee and the National Labor Relations Act, policies championed by the only Mexican-American in Congress at the time, United States Senator Dennis Chavez (New Mexico).

In an attempt to combat these and other forms of discrimination and abuse, Mexican-Americans founded the Community Service Organization (CSO) in 1947. The CSO was among the first of many organizations dedicated to improving the living and working conditions of Mexican-Americans. These efforts were precursors to the Chicano (short for "Mexicano") Movement, an intense and more successful political and cultural revolution that burgeoned with the civil rights movement of the 1960s.

The Chicano Movement (also called *El Movimiento* or *La Causa*) sought social, political, economic, and educational equality for Chicanos and hoped to increase pride in Chicano heritage and culture. Educational equality was particularly important to *La Causa* since lack of decent education deprived Chicanos of the opportunity to improve their wages and, hence, their economic standing.

On the economic front, organizations like the United Farm Workers, led by *Movimiento* hero Cesar Chávez, fought for rights of the underpaid and exploited Chicano laborers. Chávez organized successful protests, such as the California grape boycott, during which millions of Americans refused to purchase California grapes until the employers granted Chicano workers fair wages and union practices. This and many other successful boycotts and protests led to reforms, such as the Agricultural Labor Relations Act of 1974. Equally as important as the revolution on the economic front, however, was the Chicano educational revolution. Because of prejudice against the Mexican-American, Chicano students often studied in dilapidated schools with second-rate educators and materials. Young Chicanos across the country rose up and demanded a better education—better schools, better teachers, and a curriculum that acknowledged both the Chicano contribution to American society and their unique cultural heritage. Chicano student activists staged "blow-outs," sit-ins, and other such protests that eventually resulted in positive changes in curricula all across America. In addition, schools in the Southwest and elsewhere began to recruit Chicano teachers and establish programs, like bilingual education, to meet the needs of a Chicano student population.

An important "product" of *El Movimiento* was the outpouring of Chicano literature and art. Students at campuses across the nation strove to express their experiences creatively, and the number of Chicano artists—writers, musicians, painters, sculptors, and dancers—exploded. Several literary and social journals were born during this era, including *La Revista Chicano-Riquena*, a magazine that was later instrumental in encouraging Cisneros to write *The House on Mango Street*. Some of the most influential authors to emerge from the Chicano Movement include Richard Rodriguez, Tomas Rivera, Rudolfo Anaya, Luis Valdez, and Gary Soto.

But where were the women? Ironically, even as they fought with the men for equal status of their race, Mexican-American women (Chicanas) found themselves being discriminated against by their own kind. Male dominance and *machismo* are of special concern to Cisneros, whose female characters, like many Chicanas, are triply oppressed by their race, their class, and their gender. Chicanas joined together during *El Movimiento* to fight this additional form of oppression, and through their efforts they gained greater acceptance of the rights due to all Chicanas—and all women.

Today a good two-thirds of Latinos in the United States are of Mexican heritage, making Mexican-Americans the second largest minority group in America. In recent decades they have made great gains as individuals and as a community. A greater awareness of their suffering, heritage, and cultural wisdom is being shared by writers like Cisneros, whose stories bring us face to face with ghosts of America's past and redefine what it means to be an American.

Master List of Characters

Esperanza Cordero—*the narrator of the vignettes that make up the novel, a Mexican-American in her early teens who lives on Mango Street.*

Nenny (Magdalena)—*Esperanza's younger sister.*

Mama—*Esperanza's mother.*

Papa—*Esperanza's father, a hardworking laborer.*

Carlos—*Esperanza's younger brother.*

Kiki—*Esperanza's brother and the youngest Cordero child.*

Nun—*a nun from Esperanza's school who made her feel ashamed of where she lived.*

Great-grandmother—*Esperanza's great-grandmother, for whom she is named.*

Cathy—*Esperanza's neighbor, who is Esperanza's friend only for a day because her family is leaving Mango Street.*

Joe—*Esperanza's neighbor, who Cathy says is "dangerous".*

Benny and Blanca—*owners of the corner store on Mango Street.*

Edna—*owner of the big building next to Esperanza's.*

Alicia—*Esperanza's neighbor, who went to college despite many obstacles, including Alicia's father.*

Lucy and Rachel—*sisters who move to Mango Street from Texas and become friends of Esperanza and Nenny.*

Tito—*a neighborhood boy who, with his friends, later solicits kisses from Esperanza's friend Sally.*

Tito's mother—*who Esperanza runs to for help.*

Gil—*the old black man who owns the junk store, Gil's Furniture Bought and Sold, in Esperanza's neighborhood.*

Meme (Juan) Ortiz—*Esperanza's friend, whose family moved into Cathy's old house.*

Louie—*a friend of Esperanza's brother, whose family rents the basement apartment in Meme's building.*

Marin—*Louie's cousin from Puerto Rico, who is a few years older than Esperanza and "knows lots of things".*

Louie's other cousin—*Louie's male cousin, who comes to Mango Street in an expensive Cadillac and is arrested.*

Davey the Baby, his brother and sister—*residents of Esperanza's neighborhood.*

Fat Boy—*a resident of Esperanza's neighborhood.*

The Vargas kids—Eddie, Angel, Refugia, Efren and others—*the numerous, out of control children of Rosa Vargas, who live in Esperanza's neighborhood and whose father deserted them.*

Darius—*a boy in Esperanza's neighborhood.*

The Family of Little Feet—*a family in Esperanza's neighborhood, whose mother gives Esperanza, Nenny, Lucy, and Rachel old high-heeled shoes.*

Bum man—*a bum in front of a local tavern who offers Rachel money for a kiss.*

Gloria—*Nenny's friend, with whom Nenny eats lunch on school days.*

Nun in the canteen—*the nun in charge of the canteen at Esperanza's school.*

Sister Superior—*a nun at Esperanza's school who assumes Esperanza lives in the most run-down section of the neighborhood.*

Uncle Nacho—*Esperanza's uncle who gets her to dance at a baptism party.*

Esperanza's cousin by communion—*a "cousin" of Esperanza who watches her dance.*

Aunt Lala—*Esperanza's aunt who gets her her first job at Peter Pan Photo Finishers.*

Oriental Man—*an old man who works with Esperanza at Peter Pan and gives her an unwanted, lewd kiss.*

Aunt Lupe (Guadalupe)—*Esperanza's invalid aunt who encouraged Esperanza to write.*

Totchy and Frank—*Aunt Lupe's children.*

Elenita—*the "witch woman," or fortune teller, in Esperanza's neighborhood who tells Esperanza her fortune.*

Ernie—*Elenita's son.*

Geraldo—*a young, unidentified man, a* bracero, *who Marin meets at a dance and is killed in a hit-and-run accident.*

Ruthie—*Edna's daughter, a grown woman who is Esperanza's friend.*

Earl—*Esperanza's neighbor, a jukebox repairman who works the night shift and lives in Edna's basement apartment.*

Earl's "wife"—*a number of different women Earl brings home, possibly prostitutes.*

Sire—*a neighborhood boy who awakens Esperanza's sexuality.*

Lois—*Sire's girlfriend.*

Mamacita—*the obese wife of the man across the street from Esperanza who comes from another country—probably Mexico—and refuses to learn English.*

Mamacita's husband—*the man across the street who worked hard to bring his wife and children to Mango Street and who urges Mamacita to assimilate.*

Rafaela—*a young married woman on Mango Street whose husband locks her up in the apartment when he goes out.*

Sally—*Esperanza's classmate and friend, a beautiful, physically mature eighth grader whose father beats her and who marries to escape Mango Street and her father.*

Sally's father—*a strict, religious man who abuses Sally because he does not want her to bring shame to his family.*

Minerva—*a young mother whose husband frequently beats her and leaves her; she is friends with Esperanza and they share their poems with each other.*

Izaura and Yolanda—*friends of Esperanza's mother.*

The man (in "Red Clowns")—*an unnamed man, probably white, who rapes Esperanza at an amusement park.*

Sally's husband—*a marshmallow salesman who cuts Sally off from her family and friends.*

The Three Sisters—*Lucy and Rachel's mysterious aunts, who read Esperanza's palm and teach her an important lesson.*

Summary of the Novel

The House on Mango Street is comprised of 44 short character sketches, or stories, called vignettes. They are narrated by Esperanza, who just moved with her family to Mango Street, in the *barrio*. Esperanza hates their house on Mango Street because it is not a "real" house, like the ones she's seen on TV.

Esperanza, whose name means "hope," soon meets Lucy and Rachel, who she likes because they, too, are poor. She also meets Marin, who is wise about "women things" but is always stuck inside babysitting her cousins. She discovers the fear that outsiders have of her neighborhood, the fear that keeps their neighborhood "brown." She becomes friends with Alicia, who goes to college at night so she will not be stuck "behind a rolling pin" the rest of her life.

Lucy, Rachel, and Esperanza are given several pairs of old high-heeled shoes, which they put on and wear around the neighborhood. At first they feel beautiful and powerful, but soon they discover that the shoes are "dangerous." At school, Esperanza is humiliated by the Sister Superior, who assumes Esperanza lives in the worst house in the neighborhood.

Esperanza's Aunt Lala gets her a job at a photo store, where an old man gives her a lewd kiss. Esperanza feels bad because she and her friends, in a game, made fun of her invalid Aunt Lupe, who died shortly thereafter. Aunt Lupe had listened to Esperanza's poems and encouraged Esperanza to write.

Later, Esperanza has her fortune told by Elenita, the "witch woman." Elenita tells Esperanza that she will have "a home in the heart." Esperanza, who wants a "real" house, is disappointed by this fortune. Meanwhile, Sire, a boy in the neighborhood, awakens Esperanza's sexuality: She knows he is looking at her, and she dares to look back.

Esperanza, comparing herself to the elm trees in front of her house, says they are the only ones who understand her because they don't belong on Mango Street either. Meanwhile, Mamacita, the woman who lives across the street, refuses to learn English, and so she never leaves her apartment. Rafaela, another neighbor, is also stuck in her apartment; her husband locks her up whenever he goes out.

Esperanza befriends Sally, who is sad because everyone seems to think that because she is beautiful, she is bad. Minerva, just a few years older than they, already has children and a husband who beats her. Minerva and Esperanza share their poems with each other.

Esperanza vows that someday she will have a beautiful house and offer the attic to passing bums because she knows "how it is to be without a house." She also decides to wage a "quiet war" against traditional female roles, because she is not beautiful like Sally and Nenny.

Esperanza learns that her mother "could've been somebody," but she didn't finish school because she was ashamed of her clothes. Esperanza also learns that Sally's father often beats her. When Esperanza tries to protect Sally from the boys who are making her kiss them, Sally and the boys tell Esperanza to go away. Esperanza wants to die because she can't understand the game they're playing. Later, while waiting for Sally, who had run off with a boy, Esperanza is raped. Soon after, Sally gets married.

Then Esperanza meets the Three Sisters, Rachel and Lucy's aunts. They read Esperanza's palm and tell her that life is a circle;

that she does belong to Mango Street, forever; and that if she leaves, she must return. Later, Alicia also tells Esperanza that she belongs to Mango Street and that she must come back. Finally, Esperanza begins to tell a story "about a little girl who didn't want to belong," the story of Mango Street.

Estimated Reading Time

Although a fast reader should be able to complete the novel in an hour, perhaps even less, *The House on Mango Street* deserves to be read at a somewhat slower pace. The brevity of the vignettes, the naturalness of the narrator's voice, and the simplicity of the language make for easy and rapid reading. But this simplicity is deceptive. Though the vignettes are short, they are very rich, poetic, and full of meaning. This is a novel to be savored bite by bite, not swallowed whole. The reader would benefit from two or more short sittings of approximately 30 minutes each. If read in one sitting, the novel should be read slowly, with brief pauses between vignettes. The total reading time for the average reader should be approximately one and one-half to two and one-half hours.

The House on Mango Street

Part I: The House on Mango Street, Hairs, and Boys & Girls

New Characters:

Esperanza Cordero: *the narrator of the novel*

Nenny (Magdalena): *Esperanza's younger sister*

Mama: *Esperanza's mother*

Papa: *Esperanza's father*

Carlos: *Esperanza's younger brother*

Kiki: *Esperanza's youngest brother*

Nun: *a nun from Esperanza's school*

Summary

The House on Mango Street

Esperanza and her family have just moved to a house on Mango Street. They have lived on a number of different streets in the past, and Esperanza names as many of them as she can remember. What she remembers most, however, is moving around a lot.

This is the first house the Corderos own. Esperanza is glad that there is no landlord and that they don't have to share the backyard, but the house on Mango Street is a disappointment—it's not the kind of house she wanted.

They moved to Mango Street because the water pipes broke in their previous apartment, a run-down flat on Loomis Street, and the landlord refused to fix them. Esperanza had expected the house on Mango Street to be a "real" house: a house like the ones she'd seen on TV, the kind her mother described in bedtime stories. The house on Mango Street, however, is small, cramped, and crumbling.

Once, when the Corderos lived on Loomis Street, a nun from Esperanza's school saw her playing in front of their flat. The nun asked Esperanza where she lived, and when Esperanza pointed to the third floor of the building behind her, the nun made Esperanza feel ashamed that she lived "there." Esperanza vowed then that someday she would live in a house that she "could point to." Her parents say that the house on Mango Street is temporary, but Esperanza knows "how those things go."

Hairs

Esperanza describes how everyone in her family has different hair. Her favorite is her mother's hair, which smells like bread and makes Esperanza feel safe and warm.

Boys & Girls

To Esperanza, boys and girls seem to live in two completely different worlds. She notices that her brothers are best friends with each other and regrets that she's not best friends with Nenny, who, she says, is too young to be her friend. Instead, Esperanza feels Nenny is her "responsibility." In the meantime, Esperanza dreams of having her own best friend.

Analysis

The main conflict in "The House on Mango Street" is the clash between Esperanza's dream—the "American Dream" of owning a spacious, private, and secure house like the ones Esperanza sees on TV—and her Mango Street reality. Esperanza is forced to realize that she does not belong to the race or class of people who live in such houses. But Esperanza does not want to believe that she belongs in the house on Mango Street.

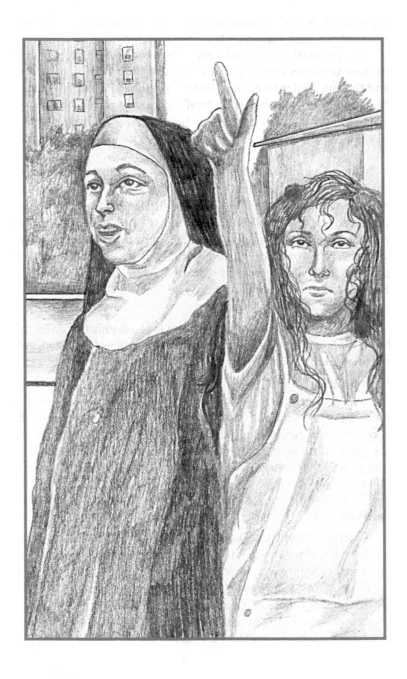

Esperanza is clearly aware of the poverty that forces the Corderos to keep moving from place to run-down place. It is also possible, if not likely, that their landlord on Loomis Street refused to fix the pipes not because the building was too old but because he wanted the Chicanos out of his building. To achieve their dream, the Corderos must struggle against both poverty and racism.

Perhaps Esperanza would not have felt so disappointed in the house on Mango Street if she had not had the encounter with the nun on Loomis Street. Ironically, it is the nun, not someone from the *barrio*, who teaches Esperanza to be ashamed of her house and makes her vow to have a "real" house one day. The word "there," which is repeated several times in this passage, sets up the conflict between "here" and "there." Esperanza is stuck here, in the *barrio*, but she wants to be there, on the other side, in the place where people have real houses.

The house is the dominant symbol throughout *The House on Mango Street*. For Esperanza, a house represents status, security, and a rise above poverty. A real house would give her privacy: It would give her a space of her own where she could forge her identity. It would be a place she could be proud of, and it would be physical evidence that she belonged somewhere. With all the moving that her family has done, Esperanza hasn't had the chance to develop a sense of place, and she feels that she doesn't belong anywhere.

It is also this moving around that has deprived Esperanza of a best friend. She envies her brothers' closeness and aches for someone to whom she can tell her secrets, someone who will understand her jokes without her "having to explain them." She feels that a best friend would release her, and without a friend—someone with whom she would be an equal—she is "a red balloon, a balloon tied to an anchor." That anchor—poverty—is holding her down, preventing her from soaring into the sky.

Cisneros meets the difficult challenge of finding a style appropriate for her young narrator, Esperanza. Esperanza is naive about some things, like boys and men, but very wise about others. By having Esperanza tell her story in many little vignettes that add up to a whole, Cisneros reflects Esperanza's reality: For her, Mango Street is a collection of stories and characters, and each story means something on its own but gains greater meaning when seen in light of the others. People are like this, too: they are valuable as individuals, but more valuable as part of a community. The stories, like the people in Esperanza's neighborhood, interact with each other, and with each interaction the stories deepen in significance. Cisneros uses a combination of poetry and storytelling to portray Esperanza's world. Cisneros' figurative and imagistic language, especially in "Hairs," makes the vignettes sound almost like poems. (Many of these stories did, in fact, start out as poems.) The windows in the house on Mango Street, for example, are "so small you'd think they were holding their breath." Esperanza's father's hair "is like a broom," and Kiki "has hair like fur"—but her mother's hair, which she likes best, takes several similes and metaphors to describe. It is "like little rosettes, like little candy circles," and it "is the warm smell of bread before you bake it."

It is significant that her mother's hair is Esperanza's favorite and makes her feel safe, for it is from her mother that Esperanza will learn her "place"—her roles as a young Chicana girl and woman. However, Esperanza's hair "never obeys barrettes or bands," and this suggests that Esperanza may not obey her mother's traditions.

The prevailing metaphor, however, is the house, which is a metaphor for the self. We live in houses like we live inside ourselves—our feelings, thoughts, and memories take up residence within us. They, too, need a house where they feel they belong. Esperanza's desire for a "real" house can thus be seen as a desire for an understanding and acceptance of the self.

Study Questions

1.   How is the house on Mango Street different from the other places Esperanza has lived?

2.   Why did the Corderos have to move from the flat on Loomis Street?

3.   What did Esperanza expect the house on Mango Street to be like?

4.   Why did Esperanza have those expectations?

5. What is the house on Mango Street like? Why isn't it "a real house"?

6. What happened between Esperanza and the nun from her school?

7. What did Esperanza realize after her experience with the nun?

8. Whose hair does Esperanza like best? Why?

9. What is Esperanza's relationship with Nenny like?

10. Does Esperanza have a best friend?

Answers

1. The house on Mango Street is different because the Corderos own it rather than rent it. They don't have to share it with anybody or answer to a landlord.

2. They had to leave the flat on Loomis because the water pipes broke and the landlord refused to fix them.

3. Esperanza expected the house on Mango Street to be a house with plenty of room, "real stairs," at least three bathrooms, and a huge yard.

4. She had these expectations because this was the kind of house she saw on TV, the kind of house her parents talked about, the kind her mother described to her in stories.

5. The house on Mango Street is small, crumbling, with no front yard, and only a small backyard. It has apartment-style stairs, only one bathroom, and only three bedrooms, so everyone has to share. It's not a house Esperanza can point to with pride.

6. The nun who passed Esperanza while she was playing in front of her flat on Loomis Street made Esperanza ashamed of where she lived. The nun made Esperanza "feel like nothing."

7. After the incident with the nun, Esperanza knew she had to have a real house, one that she "could point to" with pride.

8. She likes her mother's hair best because it smells like bread and makes her feel safe.

9. Esperanza thinks Nenny is too young to be her friend. In-
    stead, Esperanza feels that Nenny is her responsibility.

10. No, she does not, but she dreams of having one.

Suggested Essay Topics

1. Discuss Esperanza's disappointment with the house on
    Mango Street. Why doesn't she consider it "a real house"?
    What does the house represent for her?

2. Why is having a "real" house so important to Esperanza?

3. What kind of person emerges in these first three vignettes?
    What are Esperanza's concerns?

Part II: My Name, Cathy Queen of Cats, and Our Good Day

New Characters:

Cathy: *one of Esperanza's neighbors*

Joe: *man who lives next door to Cathy*

Benny and Blanca: *owners of the corner store*

Edna: *owner of the building next to Esperanza's house*

Alicia: *Esperanza's neighbor who is attending college*

Rachel and Lucy: *sisters who live across the street from Cathy*

Tito: *a neighborhood boy*

Summary

My Name

Esperanza describes the meaning and origin of her name. The
English translation is "hope," but in Spanish, she says, it means
something different, something sad. She was named after her great-
grandmother, who, like Esperanza, was born in the Chinese Year
of the Horse. That is supposed to be bad luck for women, Esperanza
is told, but she doesn't believe it. She thinks it's a lie made up by
men who "don't like their women strong."

Esperanza says she would have liked to have known her great-grandmother, a wild woman who refused to marry until her great-grandfather literally "carried her off" one day and forced her to marry him. After that, Esperanza's great-grandmother was sad and spent the rest of her life looking out the window. Esperanza worries that because she inherited her great-grandmother's name, she may also inherit her grandmother's seat by the window.

Esperanza describes how the people at school have trouble pronouncing her name. She thinks "Esperanza" is prettier than "Magdalena," but Magdalena can be shortened to Nenny, whereas Esperanza is "always Esperanza." She would like to give herself a new name that is more like the real person inside her, a name that is different, like "Zeze the X."

Cathy Queen of Cats

Esperanza meets Cathy, who tells her about some of the people in the neighborhood. Cathy agrees to be Esperanza's friend, but only for a few days—her family is moving out because the neighborhood is "getting bad." Cathy brags about being related to the queen of France, but Esperanza calls Cathy the queen of cats, since she has so many of them.

Our Good Day

Esperanza is sitting with Cathy when they are approached by Rachel and Lucy, the girls from across the street. Rachel says she will be Esperanza's best friend forever if Esperanza gives her $5, which Lucy and Rachel need to buy Tito's bike. Cathy tells Esperanza not to talk to these girls, but Esperanza likes them and gets the money for them. When she returns, Cathy is gone, but Esperanza now has two new friends and is part owner of a bike. Esperanza worries about how Rachel and Lucy will respond to her name, but they don't laugh at it. The three girls ride the bike together around the neighborhood.

Analysis

Although Esperanza's name means "hope" in English, Esperanza sees it meaning something altogether different in Spanish. In her native language, it means sadness, waiting—a longing or yearning for something past or missing rather than a hope for

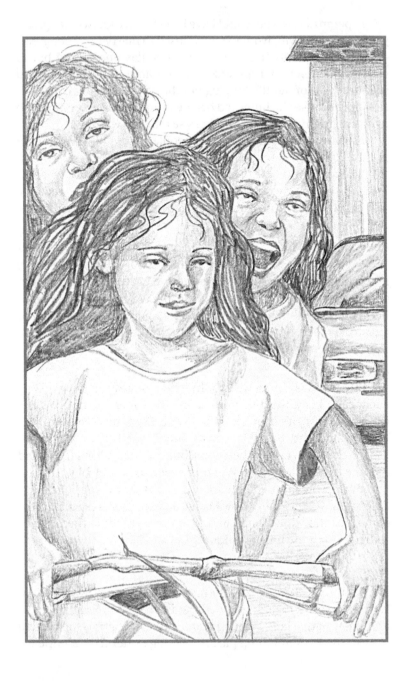

something yet to come. She compares her name to the Mexican songs her father plays, "songs like sobbing." Hearing her name in Spanish seems to build in her a longing for Mexico, a nostalgia for the time when she didn't have to worry about people laughing at her name, a time when she didn't have to worry so much about fitting in. It also carries the sadness of her great-grandmother, from whom Esperanza inherited her name.

Like her great-grandmother, Esperanza was born in the Year of the Horse. Horses are strong—and strong-willed—animals. At her young age, Esperanza is already keenly aware of the patriarchal society that wishes to rob her of this strong will and independence. She has been told that being born in the Year of the Horse is bad luck for women, but Esperanza exposes this as a lie since "the Chinese, like the Mexicans, don't like their women strong." In reality, when a woman like Esperanza's great-grandmother is born in the Year of the Horse, it is bad luck for *both* the men and the women. The men don't have the quiet, submissive wives and daughters a patriarchal society demands, and they are forced to question the legitimacy of their dominance. More importantly, the women, whose strong spirits are unable to roam free, suffer as their independence is stifled.

This is precisely what happened to Esperanza's great-grandmother. So wild that she refused to marry, utterly determined to be independent, she was at odds with her society. Eventually her society proved a stronger force: treating her like an animal, a conquest, a "fancy chandelier," Esperanza's great-grandfather literally threw her great-grandmother over his shoulder and forced her to submit to his will. Esperanza's great-grandmother could not forgive this violation of her freedom, and so "[s]he looked out the window her whole life, the way so many women sit their sadness on an elbow."

Esperanza is aware that with her name she has also inherited a history and a role, but she does not want to have the same sadness as her great-grandmother. And because her name is Esperanza, there is hope that she will not suffer the same fate.

Despite the fact that in Spanish Esperanza's name means "sadness, it means waiting"—a reference to the sadness and waiting of Esperanza's great-grandmother—it sounds much better to her when pronounced in Spanish than in English. Her teachers and classmates say her name "funny, as if the syllables were made out of tin," but in Spanish, her name is made "out of a softer something." In her native language, her name, sad as it may sound, doesn't sound awkward. It doesn't single her out as different or strange as it does in English.

Esperanza envies Nenny because her name, Magdalena—ugly as Esperanza thinks it is—can be varied. Nenny doesn't always have to be Magdalena, but Esperanza is "always Esperanza." She feels restricted by her name, as if someone else has predetermined her identity. She would therefore like to choose her own name, a name that reflects the "real" Esperanza, the one "nobody sees." However, it's not so much the name that Esperanza wants to change; it's the history and expectations that come with it. Esperanza wants to reinvent herself, and she can do so, she thinks, by giving herself a new name.

In "Cathy Queen of Cats," Esperanza finally gets herself a best friend, but it's only temporary. It has to be, because Cathy's family is moving away. Unaware of—or perhaps insensitive to—the potential insult to Esperanza, Cathy tells Esperanza that they've "got to" leave Mango Street because "the neighborhood is getting bad." The implication is that Cathy's family is moving because the neighborhood is getting too Hispanic. Cathy's claim that she is related to the queen of France indicates that she is Caucasian, and Esperanza says that Cathy's family will continue to move "a little farther away" from Mango Street each time "people like us"—poor and minority—"keep moving in."

Cathy is quick to judge, as is revealed when she tells Esperanza about some of the people in the neighborhood. Joe is a "baby-grabber" and is dangerous; Benny and Blanca are "okay"; Alicia is "stuck-up"; and Rachel and Lucy are "raggedy as rats" and, Cathy warns, "you don't want to know them." But Esperanza, unlike Cathy (who associates herself with royalty), does not feel "above" Rachel and Lucy because they're raggedy. In fact, that's precisely why she likes them.

While Cathy refuses to associate with Rachel and Lucy because of their poverty, Esperanza is drawn to them because of it. In fact, she is so strongly drawn to these two unpretentious, unprejudiced girls that she takes Nenny's money to secure their friendship. And they don't laugh at her name, which makes Esperanza like them all the more. Lucy and Rachel are from Texas, which has a very large Chicano population. Though they are probably part Chicana themselves (their last name is Guerrero, we later learn), they are "white" enough for Esperanza to fear their laughter. Still, Esperanza identifies with them and their poverty, and so the decision to choose between Cathy's friendship until next Tuesday or Rachel and Lucy's friendship (and a bike) for $5 is an easy one. Though the title of this vignette is not mentioned anywhere in the story, it is especially apt: For Esperanza, who got two new friends and part ownership of a bike, it was indeed a good day.

Study Questions

1. What does Esperanza's name mean in English and in Spanish?

2. After whom is Esperanza named?

3. What was Esperanza's great-grandmother like?

4. What kind of name would Esperanza like for herself?

5. Why will Cathy be Esperanza's friend "only till next Tuesday"?

6. Why is Cathy's family leaving the neighborhood?

7. Why does Esperanza like Lucy and Rachel?

8. Why is Cathy not waiting when Esperanza gets back from buying the bike?

9. How does Esperanza think the girls will react to her name?

10. What does Rachel do that Esperanza thinks is "sassy"?

Answers

1. Esperanza's name means "hope" in English, but "sadness or waiting" in Spanish to her.

2. Esperanza is named after her great-grandmother.

3. Esperanza's great-grandmother was a "wild" woman who was very independent until she was forced to marry. After that, she was very sad.

4. Esperanza would like a name that is more like the "real" Esperanza, the one she says "nobody sees." She would like a name that reveals who she really is, a name like "Zeze the X."

5. Cathy will be Esperanza's friend "only till next Tuesday" because that's when her family is moving away from Mango Street.

6. Cathy says her family is leaving Mango Street because "the neighborhood is getting bad." They're leaving because it is getting too populated by Mexican-Americans and other minorities.

7. Esperanza likes Lucy and Rachel because they are poor and friendly.

8. Cathy is not waiting because she dislikes Rachel and Lucy, whom Esperanza has decided to befriend.

9. Esperanza is afraid the girls will laugh at her name and wishes it was something other than "Esperanza."

10. Rachel insults a fat lady about her weight.

Suggested Essay Topics

1. Why does Esperanza want to change her name? Is it the name itself that she wants to change, or something else?

2. Discuss the difference between Cathy and the sisters Rachel and Lucy. Why does Esperanza choose to be friends with Rachel and Lucy instead of with Cathy?

Part III: Laughter, Gil's Furniture Bought & Sold, Meme Ortiz, and Louie, His Cousin & His Other Cousin

New Characters:

Gil: *owner of the junk store near Esperanza's house*

Meme Ortiz: *Juan "Meme" Ortiz, one of Esperanza's neighbors*

Louie: *one of Esperanza's neighbors*

Marin: *Louie's cousin from Puerto Rico*

Louie's other cousin: *Louie's unnamed cousin, a young man*

Summary

Laughter

Esperanza discusses her likeness to Nenny. They don't look too much alike, but they are similar in other ways, like their laughter. Esperanza describes how one day, when they were with Lucy and Rachel, they passed a house that reminded Esperanza of Mexico. Esperanza said that the house looked "like Mexico," and though Lucy and Rachel looked at her as if she were crazy, Nenny knew exactly what she meant.

Gil's Furniture Bought & Sold

Esperanza describes Gil's junk store, which she and Nenny often explore. Nenny once discovered a music box, which Gil started up for them. Though the box itself wasn't pretty, the music mesmerized the girls. Nenny tried to buy the music box, but Gil said it wasn't for sale.

Meme Ortiz

Meme, whose real name is Juan, moved into Cathy's house after she moved away. Esperanza describes Meme and his dog, who also has two names, and Meme's house, which Cathy's father built. His yard has a huge tree that the neighborhood children decided to use for a Tarzan jumping contest. Meme won the contest, but he broke both of his arms.

Louie, His Cousin & His Other Cousin

Louie, who lives downstairs from Meme, has a cousin, Marin, who lives with them and is always babysitting his little sisters. She can never come out, so she stands in the doorway, singing. Louie's other cousin only came to Mango Street once. He rode up in a big fancy Cadillac and took Esperanza and others for a ride around and around the block. Then the police came, and Louie's cousin ordered everyone out of the car. He tried to outrun the police but crashed in an alley too skinny for his Cadillac. The police hand-cuffed him and took him away.

Analysis

Esperanza's similarities to Nenny demonstrate that although two people may not look very much alike (have no visible similarity), they can be very much alike on a deeper and more profound level. The similarities that Esperanza points out are significant. First, their laughter: Both laugh "all of a sudden and surprised like a pile of dishes breaking" (a shattering, incidentally, of domestic wares). Second, they both share a past, a history—a sense of place and belonging in Mexico. Only the two of them know what Esperanza means when she says that the house "looks like Mexico." In a sense they are both outsiders, for no one else knows what they mean, but they are also insiders, for they are the only ones who understand.

Gil's store may be a "junk" store, but it is also a treasure shop, calling to mind the aphorism "one man's shack is another man's castle." Esperanza and Nenny are too poor to buy much there, but they like to go there because they can see "all kinds of things." Gil is a minority too, but of a different kind—he is black, not Hispanic, and this may explain why he "doesn't talk too much."

It is significant that the one thing Esperanza does buy from Gil is a miniature Statue of Liberty. The statue is perhaps the ultimate American symbol of independence. But even for a small replica of this statue, Esperanza must pay. It is significant that despite her poverty, she makes the purchase, indicating that she is willing to pay a price for her freedom.

The music box, too, is significant. Esperanza and Nenny are amazed at what comes out of the plain old wooden box. When Gil winds it up, "all sorts of things start happening." The music triggers something in the sisters, making them both want to buy it. Esperanza, who perhaps understands the value of such a box, assumes that she can't afford it, so she turns away and pretends not to care. She calls herself stupid, and Nenny too, for wanting something they can't have. That the music sounds like marimbas suggests that the music reminds them of Mexico, something else they can't have. Gil does not want to sell the music box; perhaps for him, too, the music connects him to a place in his past.

In "Meme Ortiz," Cisneros returns to the issue of names. Meme's real name is Juan, but he has apparently given himself another name, like Esperanza wants to do. Meme's dog also has two names, one in English and one in Spanish, which demonstrates the bilingual world of these children. Cisneros paints a vivid picture of Meme and his dog and how they run with "limbs flopping all over the place like untied shoes."

Esperanza's description of the house that Cathy's father built—slanted, crooked, and impractical (there are no closets)—reflects the way Cathy's family dealt with Mango Street. It is impractical and off-balance to keep moving away from places like Mango Street, to keep avoiding those who are different.

Esperanza's description of both the house and its yard, which is mostly dirt, reflects the poverty of the other families on Mango Street. Meme's house isn't the kind Esperanza dreams of, either. The one positive aspect of Meme's house is the tree in his backyard, from which they can see most of the neighborhood and from which Esperanza's house seems "smaller still," sitting "with its feet tucked under like a cat."

Cisneros, here and in many other vignettes, writes in "ungrammatical" constructions, like fragments. In the last paragraph of "Meme Ortiz," this type of construction effectively sets Meme's victory apart from his defeat: "Meme won. And broke both arms." It also reflects Esperanza's bilingualism, for in Spanish, it is grammatically correct to write a sentence without a subject. Translated into Spanish (*"Meme gano. Y rompio los brazos"*), this construction would be perfectly correct.

Louie's large family—Louie, his parents, his sisters, and his cousin Marin—all live crowded in the basement apartment of Meme's house. Marin is of particular interest. She's a little older than Esperanza, or at least tries to look older. She dresses to go out in dark nylons and thickly layered make-up, but, like many other women in *The House on Mango Street*, she is stuck inside. Marin is always babysitting Louie's little sisters, playing a traditional female role, but she feels trapped by it. She stands near the door of her "cage," singing songs of love.

It is the story of Louie's other cousin, however, that dominates the vignette. He drives up in a fancy, expensive Cadillac that has all the trimmings: a radio, automatic windows, and whitewalls. This is possibly the most extravagant car Esperanza and many of her neighbors had ever seen and certainly the nicest car Esperanza has ever ridden in. But the ride doesn't last long, for Louie's cousin is soon chased and arrested by the police. The fantasy is brief. Although Esperanza never tells us why Louie's cousin was arrested (perhaps she never knew), it is likely that Louie's cousin did something illegal to obtain the car. Esperanza says "we all asked for a ride and asked where he got it," but Louie's cousin doesn't answer the latter question. He also tries to outrun the police. Whether Louie's cousin stole the car or earned the money for it some other way, the police were quick to track him down and arrest him. In the end, the car, like the fantasy of someone like Louie's cousin (a Latino) owning such a car, ends up smashed: too big, it seems, to get out of Mango Street. Like Esperanza's dreams, it is big enough to get in, but too big to get out.

Study Questions

1. In what ways are Esperanza and Nenny similar?

2. What kind of store does Gil have?

3. What did Esperanza once buy from Gil?

4. What did Nenny want to buy from Gil?

5. Why couldn't she buy it?

6. Why does Esperanza say that she and Nenny are stupid for wanting the music box?

7. What is Meme's real name?

8. Why can't Marin go out?

9. What kind of car did Louie's other cousin have?

10. What happened to Louie's other cousin when he came to Mango Street?

Answers

1. Esperanza and Nenny have the same laugh and the same memories of Mexico.

2. Gil has a junk store full of used furniture and trinkets.

3. Esperanza once bought a miniature Statue of Liberty.
4. Nenny wanted to buy the music box.
5. She couldn't buy it because it wasn't for sale.
6. Esperanza says they're stupid because she knows that even if the music box were for sale, they couldn't afford it.
7. Meme's real name is Juan.
8. Marin can't go out because she's always babysitting Louie's little sisters.
9. Louie's other cousin had a yellow Cadillac.
10. The police chased him and arrested him.

Suggested Essay Topics

1. Esperanza says they only saw Louie's other cousin once, "but it was important." Why?
2. Why does Louie's other cousin get arrested? What do you think he did wrong?

Part IV: Marin, Those Who Don't, and There Was an Old Woman She Had So Many Children She Didn't Know What to Do

New Characters:

Davey the Baby, his sister and brother: *residents of Esperanza's neighborhood*

Fat Boy: *a resident of Esperanza's neighborhood*

Eddie, Refugia, Efren, Angel, and the other Vargas kids: *residents of Esperanza's neighborhood and children of Rosa Vargas*

Rosa Vargas: *a resident of Esperanza's neighborhood and a single mother*

Summary

Marin

Esperanza describes Marin, who is secretly engaged to a boy in Puerto Rico. Marin sells Avon products and is trying to save up money for her marriage. She will probably be sent back to Puerto Rico next year by Louie's parents, but Esperanza hopes not because Marin is her source of gossip and feminine advice. Marin is always babysitting, but even when she's not she is forbidden to leave the property. At night, Marin escapes to the front of the house so the boys can see her. Sometimes she dances alone under the street light, but always, it seems, she is waiting.

Those Who Don't

Esperanza notes that people "who don't know any better" expect her neighborhood to be dangerous, and they are afraid. But those who live on and near Mango Street know better, because they know each other and are comfortable in a neighborhood where everyone is "brown." Esperanza admits, however, that when they—the "brown" people—go into a neighborhood of a different color, they, too, are afraid.

There Was an Old Woman She Had So Many Children She Didn't Know What to Do

Rosa Vargas, one of Esperanza's neighbors, has too many children—many more than she can handle. Her husband left her without an explanation and without any money. The children are reckless and disrespectful. The neighbors have gotten tired of worrying about the Vargas children and have given up trying to guide them. Now the neighbors are indifferent when the Vargas children hurt themselves, even when Angel Vargas kills himself one day while "learn[ing] to fly."

Analysis

Marin is a young woman who wants to grow up fast and is waiting for an opportunity to escape Mango Street. She is trapped inside all day and at night is allowed to go only as far as the front yard. Her boundaries are clear, yet within her boundaries, she rebels. She smokes, wears make-up and short skirts, flirts unflinchingly with the neighborhood boys, and dances alone under the streetlight. She also serves as a source of feminine "wisdom" for the other girls since she is a bit older. She plans to marry her boyfriend if she goes back to Puerto Rico, and, if not, to marry a nice man she'll meet on the subway, someone who'll take her "to live in a big house far away" from Mango Street, babysitting, and boundaries. What Marin doesn't realize is that marriage brings with it its own boundaries, both figurative and literal.

Still Marin waits, Esperanza says, "for a car to stop, a star to fall, someone to change her life." Marin is waiting for someone else to take her away, for someone else to change her life, instead of making the change on her own. Unless she herself makes the change, she will spend the rest of her life waiting for the next car, the next star, the next someone.

In "Those Who Don't," the novel's second shortest vignette, Esperanza addresses two of the largest themes of the novel: stereotyping and prejudice. Esperanza notices that people "who don't know any better"—non-Hispanics—are afraid in Esperanza's neighborhood. They assume that because Hispanics are "different," they are dangerous and ready to attack strangers who enter their neighborhood. But Esperanza knows better. She knows, for example, who Fat Boy and Eddie Vargas are, and she knows they are not dangerous people. Her familiarity with the people in the neighborhood—and the color of the people in her neighborhood—takes away Esperanza's fear. Were "those who don't know better" to spend some time in her neighborhood, they would no longer be afraid.

Esperanza acknowledges this prejudice against her neighborhood, and though it makes her sad, she is not angry about it. For she realizes that she, too, is guilty of the same thing. Unfortunately, color seems to be what draws the boundaries in the neighborhoods around Mango Street. When Esperanza leaves the familiar sight of brown faces and enters "into a neighborhood of another color," she, too, is frightened. Esperanza calls those who are afraid in her neighborhood "stupid people," but she is guilty of the same "stupidity." She acknowledges the sad fact that this is, unfortunately, a part of human nature, something that has happened before, is happening now, and will continue to happen—"That is how it goes and goes." The hope is that Esperanza will learn that if others needn't be afraid in her neighborhood, she needn't be afraid in theirs. But perceptions are hard to change, and prejudice dies hard. Rosa Vargas and her children are ideal messengers for a number of ideas. First, the plight they're in reflects the plight of women (to whom the book is dedicated), particularly women who are abandoned and/or abused by their husbands. Not only does Rosa's husband leave her, but he also leaves without an explanation, without leaving money for his family, and apparently with no thought about the children. Though he's fathered so many, he refuses to take responsibility for them.

As a result, the story is not the nursery rhyme the title suggests, but a tragedy. Rosa is too poor and exhausted to take care of the children properly, and they grow up "without respect for all things living, including themselves." They risk their well-being and even their lives on silly stunts and "play." Angel, in fact, dies when he falls—or jumps—from a building or treetop. Even with Angel's death no one in the neighborhood seems to care—and therein lies the tragedy. Because of the children's utter disrespect not only for their neighbors but also for themselves, because of their disregard for anyone who tries to help them, the neighbors give up and stop worrying about and trying to protect the Vargas children. Angel falls to his death "without even an 'Oh'," and his death, sadly, will draw little more than an "Oh" from the neighbors, who have chosen, perhaps out of a sense of emotional self-preservation, not to care.

This vignette is an indictment of men like Rosa's husband, who deny their responsibility to their children and families and who, by leaving, make their children feel unwanted and unloved. It is no wonder the Vargas children have no respect for themselves—one of the people who is supposed to care for them most has deserted them, and the other is too overwhelmed with work, poverty, and grief to give them proper care.

Study Questions

1. Why does Esperanza like Marin?
2. Why is Marin saving her money?
3. Why does Marin want to get a job downtown if she stays on Mango Street?

4. According to Marin, why is it important to be out front at night?

5. Why are people who get lost in Esperanza's neighborhood afraid?

6. Why isn't Esperanza scared in her neighborhood?

7. How does Esperanza feel when she goes into a neighborhood "of another color"?

8. Why can't Rosa Vargas take care of her children?

9. What are the Vargas children like?

10. Why don't the neighbors worry about the Vargas children anymore?

Answers

1. Esperanza likes Marin because Marin "is older and knows lots of things."

2. Marin is saving her money because the boy she is engaged to in Puerto Rico hasn't gotten a job yet.

3. Marin thinks she may meet a man on the subway who will marry her and take her far away.

4. Marin says it is essential that the boys be able to see them.

5. People who get lost in her neighborhood are afraid because everyone around them is "brown," and they think that Esperanza's neighborhood is dangerous.

6. Esperanza isn't scared because she knows the people in her neighborhood, and she is comfortable being around others who are "brown."

7. Esperanza feels the way "those who don't" feel: she is nervous and scared.

8. Rosa Vargas can't take care of her children because she has too many and she is all alone and poor.

9. The Vargas children are reckless and disrespectful.

10. The neighbors don't care anymore because the Vargas children don't listen to and don't care about anyone, not even themselves.

Suggested Essay Topics

1. Esperanza says that Marin always seems to be waiting. What is she waiting for?

2. Discuss the brief vignette "Those Who Don't." What does it suggest about stereotypes and prejudice?

3. The story of Rosa Vargas and her children raises many issues—about poverty, parental responsibility, neighborly responsibility, and respect. It also shows the disastrous consequences of a combination of negative social forces. Discuss.

Part V: Alicia Who Sees Mice, Darius & the Clouds, and And Some More

New Characters:

Alicia's father: *father of Alicia, Esperanza's neighbor*

Darius: *a neighbor of Esperanza*

Summary

Alicia Who Sees Mice

Alicia's father tells her that the mice she sees while she is up studying at night don't really exist—they're just in her imagination. Besides, he says, she should be sleeping instead of studying so she can wake up early and cook for the family. Alicia's mother died, and she has had to take her mother's place at home while she attends a university across town. She is always tired because she has to travel far to the university and stays up late to study.

Darius & the Clouds

Esperanza laments the fact that there is not enough sky, butterflies, or flowers, but she is determined to make the best of it. Her neighbor, Darius, who she thinks is "a fool," says something that she thinks is simple and profound: He points to a cloud and says, "That's God."

And Some More

Esperanza, Nenny, Lucy, and Rachel have a discussion about

names: different names for snow, people, and clouds. Nenny tries to name all the clouds she sees in the sky and the others describe what the clouds look like. Lucy, Rachel, and Esperanza get into a mild fight and call each other names.

Analysis

Alicia is a pivotal character in the novel. Like Esperanza, she desires something more than the traditional role for the Chicana woman. And like Esperanza, she has tremendous obstacles to face. Because her mother has died, Alicia, the oldest, must now assume that role and has to wake up early to take care of her family. She has "inherited her mama's rolling pin and sleepiness," but "because she doesn't want to spend her whole life in a factory or behind a rolling pin," she must struggle fiercely to go to, and stay in, school. She must study late into the night—sometimes all night—beginning only after her "woman's work" is done.

Alicia's father seems to think that her studying is not right, for it may keep her from rising "early with the tortilla star" and fulfilling her household duties. Despite this pressure from her father—or perhaps because of it—Alicia perseveres. But she is afraid of her father, who denies the reality of the poverty she is trying to escape by denying the existence of the mice, which scurry "under the swollen floorboards nobody fixes." He also denies the reality of Alicia's intelligence and desire for independence by telling her she's imagining the mice.

Alicia's father represents the patriarchal system that could, in a moment, take away her opportunity to control and improve her life. Alicia is afraid that she won't be able to determine for herself what her "place" is and will end up succumbing to her father's idea of where a woman belongs. It is important that Esperanza sees Alicia as "a good girl" and a friend, for Alicia serves as an important role model for Esperanza.

"Darius & the Clouds" opens with "You can never have too much sky." The sky, with its endless, open expanse, is a symbol of freedom, of liberty, and of openness. "Here"—on Mango Street, in the urban Chicano *barrio*, in America—"there is too much sadness," Esperanza says, "and not enough sky." This is ironic because America is supposed to be the land of the free. Still, she and the other Chicanos (the "we" in this vignette) are in America now, and they will "take what [they] can get and make the best of it." Their willingness to work with the circumstances is admirable. The wisdom of Darius's statement lies in its simplicity and innocence: He notices a fat cloud in the sky and says, "That's God." Here, Darius reduces the idea of God to the simplest level: God is where we wish to see him, especially in beautiful things. The cloud is also an appropriate place to "see" God because it is ephemeral, intangible, and as omnipotent as the water of which it is made.

In "And Some More," Cisneros returns to the issues of names and language and to the cloud motif. First, Esperanza claims that the Eskimos have 30 different names for snow—a fact Lucy has a hard time accepting. But Nenny is quick to realize that classifying something into different kinds denies each element its individuality. Classifying snow, for example, denies each snowfall, and each flake, its uniqueness, and so she says there are "a million zillion kinds" of snow, "no two exactly alike." Snow is a symbol for people—though we try and try to classify them, no two people are exactly alike, and, like Nenny says, there are a million zillion different kinds. No two snowflakes—or people—are formed in exactly the same design, and no two snowfalls—or people—are exactly the same.

As for the Eskimos having 30 different names for snow, they do. This fact reveals an important function of language. Language serves as a mirror of our reality. For Eskimos, whose world is a world of snow, it is crucial for their survival that they be able to distinguish between different types of snowfall. Their language, therefore, must reflect the reality of their world. For Rachel and Lucy, who come from Texas and have very little experience with snow, it is not surprising that they only know of two kinds—clean (fresh) snow and dirty snow. Their experience with snow is limited. Lucy's simplistic view of snow, limiting it to only two narrowly defined categories, represents the view of people whose experience with the world (and with different kinds of people) is limited, and shows their readiness to categorize and limit.

Most important, however, is Nenny's insistence on giving every cloud individual status. Esperanza wants to classify clouds as cumulus and nimbus, showing off her "scientific" knowledge, but Nenny rejects this classification and says "No...That there is Nancy, otherwise known as Pig-eye." "There are all different kinds of clouds," just like there are all different kinds of people, and they cannot simply be categorized by appearance. They all deserve the dignity of a name and to be recognized as individuals, not as a type. Thus, this vignette, though it seems lighthearted and humorous, is really about the power of language to both limit and liberate—to both deny identity and grant it.

There is a noticeable lack of quotation marks and speaker cues here, which some readers may find confusing. The speaker listing the names for the clouds is Nenny, while the insults are traded by Esperanza, Lucy, and Rachel. The lack of clearly marked dialogue here helps establish this as a young writer's (Esperanza's) work, as written by someone perhaps unaware of all the written conventions of the English language. It also makes the words on the page appear less encumbered, more free. Cisneros doesn't use quotation marks in this vignette or anywhere throughout the novel, perhaps to indicate that our words don't belong to us so much as to our listeners.

Study Questions

1. Why is Alicia so tired?

2. Why is Alicia in school?

3. According to Alicia's father, where is a woman's place?

4. Why is Alicia afraid of her father?

5. Why does Darius's comment impress Esperanza?

6. What can Esperanza "never have too much" of?

7. Who is naming all the clouds in "And Some More"?

8. Why does Esperanza get mad at Rachel and Lucy?

9. According to Esperanza, how many different names for snow do the Eskimos have?

10. According to Lucy, how many different kinds of snow are there? According to Nenny?

Answers

1. Alicia is so tired because she has to travel far to school and stay up late to study.

2. Alicia is in school because "she doesn't want to spend her whole life in a factory or behind a rolling pin." She wants to have the opportunity to be more than just a housewife or a factory worker.

3. Alicia's father says a woman's place is sleeping, so she can get up early "with the tortilla star" to take care of the family.

4. Alicia is afraid of her father because he thinks she should be at home taking care of the family instead of in school studying.

5. Darius's comment impresses Esperanza because he "made it simple."

6. Esperanza says she can never have too much sky.

7. Nenny is naming the clouds.

8. Esperanza gets mad at them because they insult her mother.

9. Esperanza says they have 30 different names for snow.

10. Lucy says there are only two different kinds—clean and dirty. Nenny says there are a "million zillion" kinds.

Suggested Essay Topics

1. Discuss Alicia's predicament. What is she trying to overcome and accomplish?

2. Discuss the significance of names and all the naming that takes place in "And Some More." Why are names so important? What do they represent?

Part VI: The Family of Little Feet and A Rice Sandwich

New Characters:

The Family of Little Feet: Grandpa, Grandma, Baby, and Mother: *a family in Esperanza's neighborhood*

Bum man: *a drunkard outside the local tavern*

Gloria: *Nenny's friend*

Nun: *the nun in charge of the canteen at Esperanza's school*

Sister Superior: *the nun in charge at Esperanza's school*

Summary

The Family of Little Feet

Esperanza describes the small feet of a family in her neighborhood. The mother of that family gives Esperanza, Rachel, and Lucy three pairs of old high-heeled shoes.

Because the mother has small feet, the shoes fit the girls perfectly. They put on the shoes and take off their socks to reveal their legs. They walk down to the corner in the shoes, practicing how to walk in high heels. On the corner, the men stare at them, and Mr. Benny tells them such shoes "are dangerous." He threatens to call the cops, but the girls run.

On the avenue, a boy makes a suggestive comment to them. Rachel asks Esperanza and Lucy if they like these shoes, and they all agree that they're the best shoes of all. In front of the local bar, Rachel asks a drunk man on the stoop if he likes their shoes. He says yes and flatters Rachel, who is intoxicated by all the attention she has gotten in the shoes. He offers Rachel a dollar for a kiss, and she considers it. Lucy quickly pulls her away, and they run back to Mango Street where they take off the shoes and hide them.

A Rice Sandwich

Esperanza wants to eat lunch in the school's canteen, where the "special kids," the ones who can't go home for lunch, eat. She begs her mother to write a note permitting her to stay in the canteen instead of walking home for lunch. Esperanza's mother is reluctant

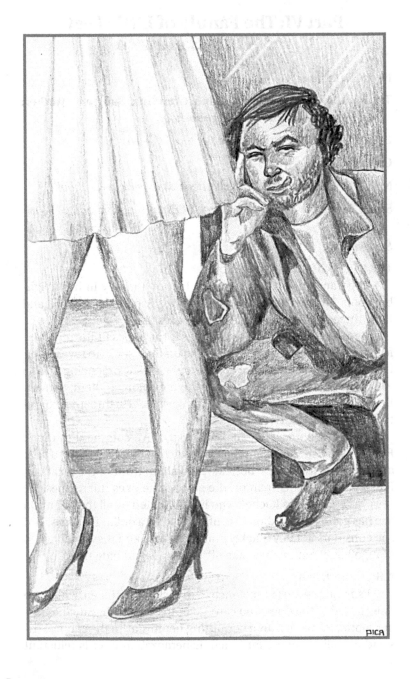

because packing lunch is more work for her, but Esperanza is persistent and finally convinces her mother to write the note.

At lunch time the next day Esperanza is sent to Sister Superior who must approve of Esperanza's request. Sister Superior tells Esperanza that she doesn't live too far to walk and she shouldn't eat at school. She tells Esperanza to come to the window to point out her house but doesn't give Esperanza the chance to do so. Instead, Sister Superior points to the ugliest houses in the neighborhood and assumes Esperanza lives there. Esperanza, because she is upset, simply nods "yes" and begins to cry. Sister Superior lets Esperanza eat in the canteen that day only, and Esperanza cries while she eats a greasy, cold rice sandwich.

Analysis

In "The Family of Little Feet," the girls suddenly discover the power—and danger—of their sexuality. The high-heeled shoes make them look and feel like the women they will soon become. Sassy, young Rachel masters the art of strutting in the heels and teaches the others how to make their bodies and shoes "talk."

Already elated by their self-discovery (they've just learned that they "have legs...good to look at, and long"), they are further buoyed by the stares of the men on the corner. Mr. Benny warns them of the dangers of such shoes, but the girls are drunk on the attention they're getting—so drunk, in fact, that Rachel cannot recognize the lewdness of the bum man's offer. Lucy and Esperanza do, however, and they run back to Mango Street "the back way," afraid now of what the shoes have gotten them into. Clearly they do not know how to handle their newly discovered sexuality. They realize the "baggage" that comes along with a certain way of dressing and that those shoes, especially on ones so young, set up certain expectations and perceptions about the wearer's experience and availability. That is why "no one complains" when Lucy's mother throws the shoes away.

This vignette opens with vivid imagery describing the family of little feet. (Noticeably, there is no father in this family.) Grandpa's feet are "fat and doughy like thick tamales"; Grandma's are "lovely as pink pearls"; the baby's are "pale see-thru like a salamander's"; and the mother's feet "descended like white pigeons."

This focus on feet—on the part of our body that connects us to the ground—calls attention to a body part that we often overlook, but whose adornment can alter us greatly. That shoes so change the girls also reveals how much our dress determines how others treat and perceive us—and how we treat and perceive ourselves.

In "A Rice Sandwich," Esperanza believes the kids in the canteen—because they wear keys around their necks—are special. "Even the name sounds important," she says. In reality, the kids eat there because there is no one at home for them during the day or because they live too far away to walk. Esperanza, however, desperately wants to belong to something, and she sees not a sad group of latchkey children but a select group of children who get special treatment every day.

After she finally convinces her mother to write the permission note, Esperanza goes to school with a rice sandwich—they're too poor to afford lunch meat. When Esperanza seeks permission from Sister Superior, however, her dreams of belonging are shattered. Sister Superior assumes Esperanza's house is only a few blocks away, in the worst part of the neighborhood, in the houses that "even the raggedy men are ashamed to go into." For Esperanza, it is bad enough that she lives on Mango Street; now Sister Superior assumes that she lives in even more shameful conditions. Esperanza doesn't protest ; instead, she just nods and cries. This is because she feels as if she is condemned both by the reality of her house on Mango Street and the judgment of those who live outside the *barrio*. Even if she did point out the right house, she would still be ashamed.

Later, in the canteen, Esperanza doesn't feel the way she had hoped to—she doesn't feel like she belongs. Instead, the others watch her as she cries and eats her cold, greasy sandwich. She realizes that the canteen is, after all, "nothing special," and she goes home ashamed of her ethnicity and more ashamed of her house and her poverty than ever.

Study Questions

1. Where do Rachel, Lucy, and Esperanza get the high-heeled shoes?

2. What does Mr. Benny say about their shoes?

3. What does the bum man offer Rachel?

4. Why do the girls hide the shoes when they come home?

5. Why does Esperanza want to eat in the canteen?

6. How does Esperanza convince her mother to write the permission note?

7. What does Nenny do for lunch?

8. Why doesn't Sister Superior let Esperanza have lunches in the canteen?

9. Why does Sister Superior assume Esperanza lives in the ugly three-flats?

10. Was the canteen what Esperanza expected?

Answers

1. They get the shoes from the mother of the Family of Little Feet.

2. Mr. Benny says those shoes are dangerous.

3. The bum man offers Rachel $1.00 for a kiss.

4. The girls hide the shoes because they are "tired of being beautiful" and aren't ready to handle it.

5. Esperanza wants to eat in the canteen because she thinks the kids who eat there are "special."

6. For three days in a row, she tells her mother that she is too skinny and that her mother will appreciate her more if she's not home for lunch every day.

7. Nenny goes to her friend Gloria's, where they watch cartoons.

8. Sister Superior says Esperanza lives too close to school to have to stay for lunch.

9. Sister Superior assumes that because Esperanza is Chicana, she is poor and lives in the worst conditions.

10. No, the canteen has nothing special about it.

Suggested Essay Topics

1. Discuss what happens to the girls when they walk around in high heels. What "power" do they discover? Why do they get "tired of being beautiful" so quickly?

2. Discuss what happens to Esperanza in Sister Superior's office. Why does Sister Superior assume that Esperanza lives in the worst part of the neighborhood? Why doesn't Esperanza show Sister Superior where she really lives?

Part VII: Chanclas, Hips, and The First Job

New Characters:

Uncle Nacho: *Esperanza's uncle*

Esperanza's cousin by communion: *a boy Esperanza knows through church*

Aunt Lala: *Esperanza's aunt*

Oriental man: *a man who works with Esperanza at Peter Pan Photo Finishers*

Summary

Chanclas

Esperanza's mother comes home from buying new clothes for the family to wear to Esperanza's cousin's baptism party. Esperanza gets a beautiful new dress and slip, but her mother forgot to buy her new shoes. Uncle Nacho takes them to the church, where everyone seems to be having a good time except Esperanza. She feels stupid in her new dress and old shoes.

Esperanza's cousin by communion asks her to dance, but she says no because she is too self-conscious about her shoes. Then Uncle Nacho convinces her to dance, and even though at first she's very worried about her shoes, she soon forgets about them and enjoys herself dancing. Everyone watches them dance and applauds when they finish. Esperanza is proud, and she is also aware that her cousin watches her dance the rest of the night.

Hips

Esperanza, Nenny, Lucy, and Rachel play double dutch and talk about hips. Nenny says something Esperanza thinks is stupid, but Esperanza agrees with Nenny so that Lucy and Rachel won't make fun of her little sister. Esperanza repeats with authority facts about hips she's learned from Alicia and says that they need to know what to do with their hips once they get them. Esperanza, Lucy, and Rachel practice shaking their hips and make up songs about hips for their double dutch game. Nenny, however, is lost in her own thoughts about babies and sings an old song instead of making up a new one about hips.

The First Job

Esperanza decides to get a job because she needs money to help pay for Catholic high school. Before she even starts looking, however, her Aunt Lala gets her a job. Esperanza, who must lie about her age, starts the job the next day.

Esperanza's job is easy, but she is self-conscious and shy. She is afraid to eat with strangers in the lunchroom, so she eats her lunch in the bathroom. At break time, she sits in the coatroom where she meets an older Oriental man. He talks with her for a while and makes her feel less alone. Then he tells her it's his birthday and asks her for a kiss. Esperanza tries to kiss him on the cheek, but he grabs her face and forces a long kiss on the lips.

Analysis

Chanclas, which translates as "old shoes," also has the Spanish-American meaning of "good for nothing," which is exactly how Esperanza feels at the baptism party in her new dress and old shoes.

The contrast between these shoes and the high heels she wore earlier is striking. Where the high heels at first made her confidence soar, her *chanclas* make her self-esteem plummet. The two pairs of shoes elicit two very different emotions in Esperanza: sensuality and shame. This chapter is important because Esperanza learns, with the help of Uncle Nacho, to overcome that shame. Whereas earlier the shoes themselves were what made her feel attractive, here, once she forgets about her shoes and begins to dance, she herself begins to feel attractive. The shoes become incidental, not elemental, to her beauty. Her cousin by communion watches Esperanza all night, and she is acutely aware of his eyes on her—and acutely aware of her blossoming sexuality.

Esperanza's emerging sexuality is also the subject of "Hips." Hips are the only bones on the skeleton that distinguish women from men (a fact, like many others, that Esperanza learns from Alicia). Hips are, therefore, an all-important feature; they are what separates women from men, and they serve as a physical dividing line between the genders. By acknowledging the importance of hips and practicing the "shake," the girls are acknowledging the literal sway that female hips have over boys and men.

At least, this is what Esperanza, Lucy, and Rachel are thinking about. Nenny, "because of her age," is thinking about hips and the babies that come from them, not about hips and the men that are attracted to them. And so she doesn't make up a song about hips like the other girls do.

Nenny is not troubled by—and apparently not even aware of—the disappointment of the other girls when Nenny starts to sing a familiar song. That's because Nenny is "too many light years away," Esperanza explains. "She is in a world we don't belong to anymore"—the world before hips. Ironically, it is Nenny, the least physically mature, who says the most mature thing about hips—that women sway their hips to rock the baby inside to sleep. While the other girls worry about seduction, Nenny is concerned only with reproduction.

While "Hips" and "Chanclas" are not excessively descriptive, they are notable for their attention to details: The chair Esperanza sits in at the church is "a metal folding chair stamped Precious Blood"; her new slip has "a little rose on it"; Nenny is wearing "the little gold earrings our mama gave her for her first Holy Communion." In "Hips," Cisneros also includes the lyrics to the girls' songs and a series of vivid metaphors and similes to describe hips and Nenny. Hips are "[r]eady and waiting like a new Buick with the keys in the ignition" (though it is important to note that Esperanza asks, "Ready to take you where?"). Hips "bloom like roses," and in Esperanza's song they are "skinny like chicken lips" and "baggy like soggy band-aids." The double-dutch ropes "open wide like jaws"—and like hips—for Nenny, who is "the color of a bar of naptha laundry soap, she is like the little brown piece left at the end of the wash, the hard little bone."

On the heels of this vignette dedicated to hips comes Esperanza's first real experience of what can happen to her now that she's on the verge of getting them. At her new job, Esperanza is hesitant to assert herself. She is insecure and afraid to eat with strangers, so she hides herself in a bathroom stall for her meal. No one makes an attempt to befriend her except the Oriental man, who is himself a minority.

However, his intentions are none too admirable. He is friendly to Esperanza so that she will like him and trust him, and once he gains her trust, he takes advantage of her. He knows that she doesn't perceive him as a threat because he is nice to her and because he is old. He also knows that she is naive and innocent and easily taken advantage of. Esperanza learns that male sexuality is often asserted by force, not by sway, and that there are moments when she may be at its mercy. Unfortunately, this is a mere precursor of things to come.

It is interesting that Esperanza tells us what happens but does not tell us how she feels about the incident. By ending the vignette abruptly with the unwanted kiss, the reader is able to feel both Esperanza's shock and discomfort. It is an experience that leaves her speechless, too surprised and ashamed for words.

Study Questions

1. What occasion is Esperanza's family celebrating in "Chanclas"?
2. Why does Esperanza not want to dance?
3. Who finally gets Esperanza to dance?
4. Who watches Esperanza dance all night?
5. Why does Esperanza agree with the stupid thing that Nenny says?
6. In what way are hips "scientific"?
7. What does Nenny say swaying one's hips is for?
8. What is Esperanza's first job?
9. Why doesn't Esperanza eat lunch in the lunchroom?
10. What happens with the Oriental man?

Answers

1. They are celebrating her cousin's baptism.
2. Esperanza doesn't want to dance because she's embarrassed about her shoes.
3. Esperanza's Uncle Nacho finally gets her to dance.
4. Esperanza's cousin by communion watches her dance all night.
5. Esperanza agrees with Nenny so that Lucy and Rachel won't laugh at Nenny.
6. Hips are scientific because they are the skeletal bones that distinguish men from women.
7. Nenny says hips are for lullabying the baby inside to sleep.
8. Esperanza's first job is matching photographs with their negatives.
9. Esperanza doesn't eat in the lunchroom because she is afraid to eat alone among strangers.
10. The Oriental man forces Esperanza to give him a lewd kiss.

Suggested Essay Topics

1. Discuss Esperanza's emotions that night at the baptism party. Why was she ashamed? What made her forget about her old shoes?
2. Consider what happens to Esperanza on her first day on the job. How did the Oriental man violate her trust? How do you think this event affects Esperanza?

Part VIII: Papa Who Wakes Up Tired in the Dark, Born Bad, and Elenita, Cards, Palm, Water

New Characters:

Aunt Guadalupe (Aunt Lupe): *Esperanza's invalid aunt*

Frank and Totchy: *Aunt Lupe's children*

Elenita: *a fortune teller in Esperanza's neighborhood*

Ernie: *Elenita's son*

Summary

Papa Who Wakes Up Tired in the Dark

Esperanza's father wakes her up early one morning to tell her that her grandfather has died. She is the first child he tells because she is the oldest, and she will have to tell the others. Esperanza wonders what she would do if she lost her father, who is always up and off to work before they even wake up. She has never seen him cry before, and she takes him into her arms and holds him.

Born Bad

Esperanza claims that she'll probably go to hell and that she deserves to go because she was "born on an evil day" and because she, Rachel, and Lucy made fun of her Aunt Lupe, an invalid, who died soon after.

Aunt Lupe had been sick for a long time, but from old photographs Esperanza knew Aunt Lupe used to be strong and pretty. Esperanza wonders why Aunt Lupe was chosen to "go bad" and acknowledges the indiscriminate nature of disease.

Esperanza, Lucy, and Rachel liked Aunt Lupe. Esperanza often read library books to her aunt. Once, Esperanza recalls with shame, she tried to show Aunt Lupe a picture in one of her books. She didn't realize that Aunt Lupe was blind.

Aunt Lupe also listened to Esperanza's own stories and poems, and she encouraged Esperanza to keep writing. Still, they had become so used to Aunt Lupe's illness that it was "easy" to imitate her in their mimicking game.

Elenita, Cards, Palm, Water

Esperanza goes to Elenita's house to get her fortune told. Esperanza, who has been there before, fills up a glass with water for Elenita to look into. Elenita also reads Esperanza's palm and a deck of cards. She tells Esperanza's fortune: She will go to a wedding soon, and she has lost an anchor of arms. Esperanza asks Elenita about a house, because that's what she really wants to know. Elenita answers that Esperanza will find "a home in the heart." Esperanza doesn't understand what this means.

Analysis

Often it is difficult for us to accept that someone we love has died, and sometimes the loss doesn't become real for us until we articulate it to others. That is what happens with Esperanza's father, the "brave" man who suddenly "crumples like a coat and cries" when he tells Esperanza about his father.

Esperanza's father has not been a prominent figure in the novel thus far (her mother has been a much stronger presence), but we realize, as does Esperanza, that her father is very important to her. He may be *macho* (this is the first time Esperanza has seen him cry), but he is also a hard worker. Every morning he "wakes up tired" and leaves before the children awake, already off to work a long, demanding day that leaves him exhausted. Though he is *macho*, he doesn't seem to believe in *machismo*—he doesn't imprison his daughter or wife like other men in the novel do.

The death of someone else's father makes Esperanza realize— as death so often does—how much her own father means to her. She must also realize she is lucky to have the kind of father she has.

In "Born Bad," Esperanza tells the story of the death of someone else who was very important to her. "Born Bad" is one of the longest vignettes in *The House on Mango Street* and also one of the most descriptive. It is the only vignette that includes a sample of Esperanza's poetry.

Esperanza draws a sharp contrast between the Aunt Lupe that was—the strong, pretty, "[g]ood to look at" swimmer—and the Aunt Lupe that is: a sickly, blind "little oyster, a little piece of meat on an open shell." Esperanza feels a great deal of guilt for making fun of Aunt Lupe, especially because Aunt Lupe died soon afterwards; but her reason for telling this story is not to absolve herself of the guilt. Rather, she is trying to understand why Aunt Lupe had been chosen to "go bad" in the first place.

The cause of Aunt Lupe's illness is speculative at best—Esperanza provides many "maybe's" and some "might have been's"—but "[there] was no evil in her birth." Esperanza comes to the remarkably mature and accurate conclusion that "diseases have no eyes. They pick with a dizzy finger anyone, just anyone." Some people may, of course, be more predisposed to certain illnesses than others, but Esperanza recognizes that no matter how good we are or how careful we are, nothing can protect us from the random nature of disease.

Esperanza realizes that Aunt Lupe had been a positive force in her life. She had always listened to Esperanza read, whether the stories and poems were Esperanza's own or from the library. More importantly, Aunt Lupe is the only character so far who encouraged Esperanza to write.

Esperanza's poem reflects her desire to be someone else, her dissatisfaction with herself ("but I'm me," she laments). She desires to be "like the waves on the sea, / like the clouds in the wind," two natural forces that are ever moving and changing. Waves and clouds are constantly redefining themselves, always shifting their shape and altering their movements. Esperanza doesn't want to be held to one way of being.

Aunt Lupe encourages Esperanza to keep writing—in fact, she tells Esperanza, "you must keep writing. It will keep you free." Though Esperanza confesses she didn't know what Aunt Lupe meant at the time, this book is evidence that she eventually understood. Aunt Lupe knew the power that words, shaped into stories and poems, have to keep us free from what hurts and haunts us.

The vignette concludes with a cryptic "And then we began to dream the dreams." There is no further reference to these dreams, so the reader is left to decide on his or her own what Esperanza means. The dreams are likely dreams about Aunt Lupe, dreams brought on by guilt. Esperanza's guilt is, of course, heightened by the fact that her mother is superstitious. Her mother claims Esperanza was born "on an evil day," so it is likely that she fears some sort of retribution for what they did to Aunt Lupe.

Esperanza has inherited some of her mother's superstition and is a regular customer of Elenita, the "witch woman." Elenita's home-made brand of fortune-telling (for example, "reading" warm tap water in a glass with a beer slogan on it) suggests at first that she may be something of a quack, but her fortune is more accurate than Esperanza could have hoped for. Esperanza doesn't—and perhaps the reader doesn't—understand the significance of "a home in the heart" at first, but this phrase is the key to Esperanza's happiness.

Esperanza's greatest longing since the beginning of the novel has been for a house of her own, a house of which she will be proud rather than ashamed. Elenita's fortune suggests that Esperanza's house will not be a house outside of her, one that Esperanza will inhabit, but rather a house inside of her. Compared to Elenita's superstitious remedies like rubbing "a cold egg across your face" to get rid of a headache and her cliche fortune "You will go to a wedding soon," this is remarkably insightful. It is only within her heart—within herself—that Esperanza will find her true home. A "real" house is not something material, but rather something spiritual: A home in the heart means being at home with, comfortable with, one's self and one's identity. When one's home is in the heart, one can be "at home" anywhere.

Study Questions

1. Whose funeral must Esperanza's father attend?
2. Why does Esperanza hold her father?
3. Why does Esperanza think she will go to hell?
4. What is Esperanza's theory about disease?
5. What does Esperanza discover when she reads *The Water-babies* to her aunt?
6. What does Aunt Lupe say to Esperanza about writing?
7. What does Esperanza wish she could do while Elenita is getting ready?
8. What interrupts Elenita while she is telling Esperanza's fortune?

9. How much does Esperanza pay for her fortune?

10. What does Elenita tell Esperanza about her future?

Answers

1. He is going to his father's funeral.

2. Esperanza holds him because she realizes how much she loves him.

3. Esperanza thinks she will go to hell because she was born on a "bad day" and because she made fun of Aunt Lupe.

4. Esperanza believes that disease is indiscriminate—it can attack anyone at any time for no reason.

5. Esperanza discovers that her aunt is blind.

6. Aunt Lupe tells Esperanza to keep writing because writing will keep her free.

7. Esperanza wishes she could go into the living room and watch *Bugs Bunny* with Ernie.

8. Elenita is interrupted by the kids' fighting.

9. Esperanza pays $5.00.

10. Elenita tells Esperanza that she will go to a wedding, that she has lost an anchor of arms, and that she will have a home in the heart.

Suggested Essay Topics

1. Aunt Lupe tells Esperanza that writing "will keep you free." Consider this statement. What does Aunt Lupe mean? How can writing keep someone free?

2. What does Elenita mean by "a home in the heart"? Discuss the significance of this statement.

Part IX: Geraldo No Last Name, Edna's Ruthie, The Earl of Tennessee, and Sire

New Characters:

Geraldo: *a young man Marin meets at a dance*

Ruthie: *Edna's daughter*

Earl: *the man who lives in Edna's basement*

Earl's "wife": *the different women Earl brings home*

Sire: *a neighborhood boy*

Lois: *Sire's girlfriend*

Summary

Geraldo No Last Name

Marin meets Geraldo, a young Hispanic man, at a dance. He dies later that evening in a hit-and-run accident. No one seems to know anything about him, and no one seems to understand why Marin is so upset if she only met him that evening. Geraldo was a wetback, a temporary and probably illegal immigrant worker who didn't speak any English and didn't have any identification. No one even knew his last name or where he lived. No one, in fact, knew that he worked hard and sent his money home to his family. Those he left behind in his native country will never know what happened to him.

Edna's Ruthie

Ruthie, Edna's daughter, is the only "grown-up" Esperanza knows who "likes to play." She laughs to herself, whistles beautifully, and is frightened inside stores. She has the ability to see beauty in common and unusual things, but she is also very indecisive. Once her mother's friends invited her to join them for some bingo. Ruthie couldn't decide whether or not to go, and after 15 minutes they left without her.

Ruthie says she is married, and Esperanza can't understand why Ruthie is with her mother on Mango Street if she has a house and a husband outside the city. Ruthie keeps telling Esperanza that her husband is coming to get her, but he never comes.

The Earl of Tennessee

Earl rents the basement apartment in Edna's building next door. He works at night, has a large record collection, and often gives records away to Esperanza and her friends. The neighbors say Earl has a wife, but those who've seen her don't seem to be describing the same woman.

Sire

Esperanza notices that Sire, a boy from her neighborhood, has been watching her. Once she returned his stare and it made her feel wonderful to have someone look at her "like that." Her parents tell her to stay away from him because he's a "punk."

  · Then Esperanza sees Sire with his girlfriend, Lois. She watches them together and wonders what they do when they're alone. Esperanza expresses a desire to explore her sexuality, to do "bad" things instead of just thinking about them.

Analysis

"Geraldo" is the tragic story of the death of an immigrant. Geraldo, whom Marin meets at a dance, is young, "pretty," and works in a restaurant. That's all Marin knows of him.

Because Marin is so upset by Geraldo's death, those investigating the accident have a hard time believing that's all Marin knows about him and that they only just met that evening. They are surprised that Marin stayed "for hours and hours, for somebody she didn't even know."

Though it is possible that Marin had met Geraldo before, the more likely conclusion is that Marin is upset because Geraldo is Hispanic, like her, and his death will go unmourned. They ask Marin "What does it matter?" But it does matter. To the authorities, who see Geraldo as "just another wetback," his death is meaningless. Because he is Hispanic and because he appears to be an illegal alien (he has no identification), his death may even be welcome to them.

But in Marin's eyes, Geraldo represents the thousands of *braceros* and wetbacks who, like Geraldo, have come to the United

States to find work and a better life for themselves and their families. Esperanza imagines the tiny rooms Geraldo rented and the money he sent home to his family. She also imagines his family back home thinking that he'd deserted them, wondering why they never heard from him again. His life and work, in short, will go unappreciated. He dies slandered as a wetback rather than respected as a hardworking, family-oriented young man.

Ruthie is unique among the characters that populate Mango Street. She is the "only grown-up who still likes to play," but not because she has a childlike disposition. Rather, it seems, Ruthie has some sort of disability that has left her stuck at a certain age of emotional development. Ruthie just appeared one day, Esperanza says, which may suggest she had been in an institution of some sort. While this is somewhat speculative, what is certain is that the husband Ruthie talks of either does not exist or has abandoned her.

Ruthie has a difficult time functioning in society: She is petrified by stores and decisions and has a rather short attention span. She is special to Esperanza because, like a child, she "sees lovely things everywhere." She also shares Esperanza's passion for books, but she cannot read them. She seems to have several ailments that she never takes care of, so it's unclear if they are real or imaginary.

Earl is another interesting character. Like Ruthie, he is not thematically significant, but he is interesting all the same. He lives in an apartment that smells of "mold and dampness, like books that have been left out in the rain." His dogs don't just walk; they "leap and somersault like an apostrophe and comma." These descriptions, in which Esperanza uses two similes that refer to writing, show how important words and writing are in Esperanza's world.

The most interesting thing about Earl is not him but his "wife." Everyone who has seen her gives a different account of what she looks like. Though no one directly says it, Earl's "wife" is no wife at all but rather a series of women he brings home, women who "never stay long." They always "walk fast into his apartment," perhaps because Edna, who is notorious for evicting tenants, just might evict Earl for such questionable behavior.

Sire is the "punk" who awakens Esperanza's sexual desire. She notices him looking at her and his look makes her "blood freeze."

She watches Lois, the kind of girl who goes "into alleys," with interest to see what it is about her that Sire likes.

Esperanza is at the age where she is "waiting to explode"—she's ready to experiment, to discover. She wants to be out there with the boys, but she is on the "wrong" side—inside, not outside; imagining, not doing. The closing questions lead Esperanza into a daydream about what it would be like to kiss Sire, which suggests that Esperanza has not yet been kissed by a boy.

In this vignette, "the trees" are mentioned twice. First, they talk to themselves, saying "wait, wait, wait." The message, however, is clearly for Esperanza, who should wait before she decides to do the kind of things she dreams about with someone like Sire. Second, Esperanza spends her evenings "talking to the trees" outside her window instead of to the boys on the street. These trees are the four skinny trees of the next vignette.

Study Questions

1. Where does Marin meet Geraldo?

2. How does Geraldo die?

3. Why can't the authorities notify anyone about Geraldo's death?

4. What is special about Ruthie?

5. Why doesn't Ruthie go with Edna's friends to play bingo?

6. What does Earl do for a living?

7. What does Earl's wife look like?

8. What happens when Esperanza looked back at Sire?

9. According to Esperanza's parents, what kind of boy is Sire? What kind of girl is Lois?

10. What does Esperanza want to do at night?

Answers

1. Marin meets Geraldo at a dance.

2. Geraldo dies in a hit-and-run accident.

3. They can't notify anyone because Geraldo doesn't have any identification.

4. Ruthie is an adult who still likes to play. She also sees beauty in ordinary things.

5. Ruthie doesn't go because she can't decide if she should go or not.

6. Earl is a jukebox repairman.

7. Earl's "wife" looks different depending on who saw her.

8. Sire, who is riding his bike, bumps into a parked car.

9. Esperanza's parents say Sire is a punk, and Lois is like the girls who "go into alleys."

10. Esperanza would like to actually be outside with a boy instead of just dreaming about it.

Suggested Essay Topics

1. Discuss the story of Geraldo. Why is his death so tragic? Why is Marin so upset by it?

2. Discuss what Esperanza is going through in "Sire." Why is this "punk" so important to her? What does he awaken in her?

Part X: Four Skinny Trees and No Speak English

New Characters:

Mamacita and her husband: *neighbors who live across the street from Esperanza*

Summary

Four Skinny Trees

Esperanza describes the four skinny trees outside her window. The trees, she says, are the only ones who understand her, and she

is the only one who understands them. Like her, they have been put on Mango Street where they don't belong. The trees are skinny but strong, with deep roots, and they talk to Esperanza while she sleeps. When she feels weak, she gains strength by looking at the trees.

No Speak English

Mamacita, the obese wife of the man across the street, finally comes from somewhere in Latin America to be with her husband. He had worked very hard to earn enough money to bring her and their son to Mango Street. Mamacita is so big that they literally have to push and pull her out of the taxicab.

After her arrival, however, no one sees Mamacita outside anymore. Some say she doesn't come out because she's too fat, others because there's too many stairs to climb; but Esperanza thinks it's because Mamacita can't speak English. Mamacita just sits inside by the window and sings songs about her native country. She is very sad and wants to go home. Her husband gets very angry about this because to him, Mango Street is home. He urges her to learn English, but she won't. Her heart breaks when their child learns to speak English by watching TV.

Analysis

The four skinny trees are a source of inspiration for Esperanza. More than any person or thing so far in the novel, the four trees give Esperanza strength and encouragement. This is because Esperanza sees herself in them, and them in her. The likeness is more than physical. Though they also have "skinny necks and pointy elbows," the other similarities are more significant.

Like Esperanza, the trees do not belong on Mango Street. They belong somewhere else, somewhere better, somewhere with more room to grow; but, like Esperanza, they have been put on Mango Street against their will. Though they are skinny, they are strong—strong enough to grow even though they are surrounded by concrete instead of grass. Likewise, Esperanza is strong enough to grow in an environment in which she is restricted by her race, class, and gender.

What makes the trees—and Esperanza—strong is their roots, which are an important symbol. The trees' roots are "ferocious," and the trees "grow up and they grow down and grab the earth between their hairy toes and bite the sky with violent teeth and never quit their anger." The trees hold on to earth and reach for the sky with all the strength that Esperanza holds on to her anger— anger at being surrounded by the concrete that is Mango Street.

There are four trees, but they are all of one piece. If one tree "forget[s] his reason for being, they'd all droop." All four must work to keep the others strong. Though Esperanza may not understand this yet, the trees are like the ideal community: the weakness of one weakens them all, for they are all one being. The trees understand that the welfare of the others is important to the welfare of each tree in the community and that they are all responsible for the welfare of the others.

The trees are also Esperanza's teachers. "Keep, keep, keep," they tell her: keep fighting, keep dreaming, keep reaching. When Esperanza feels overwhelmed by her poverty and her lack of freedom, she looks to the trees as an example of this keeping. The trees keep growing and reaching, despite their obstacles. This is their inspiration. They remind Esperanza to keep reaching, both up and down—into the future and into the past. Like the roots below nourish the tree branches that reach into the sky, Esperanza's roots— both her immediate and distant past (her heritage)—are strong, and they provide Esperanza with the strength to keep reaching.

Significantly, no matter how high a tree may reach, it is always connected to its roots; if severed from them, it will die. Esperanza has to realize that if she tries to break her ties to Mango Street completely, her dreams, too, will perish.

Though the vivid image of an immense Mamacita being pushed and pulled out of a taxicab is humorous, the message in "No Speak English" is a serious one. Mamacita's husband had been in the United States for a long time before she arrived. He worked two jobs to save enough money for his family to join him. No matter how much Mango Street has become a home to him, however, it is a foreign place for Mamacita, who doesn't speak English. Unable to communicate with the world around her, she feels alien, isolated. It is impossible to feel at home under such circumstances.

Mamacita could learn the language, but she won't. She refuses to accept this as her new home, to accept the fact that she is no

longer in her native country. She remains inside, homesick, stuck on Mango Street. Like the other women before her, she is trapped, but not only physically. Mamacita is trapped linguistically, which keeps her physically isolated, as well, because she won't come out.

It is hard to blame Mamacita's husband for being angry with her. He had worked so hard to bring her to Mango Street, and all she wants to do is go "home." But for him, because he speaks English and has assimilated, Mango Street *is* home. The question that arises, then, is what makes a "home"? For Mamacita, the answer is clear: Home is not where she lives, but where her heart is.

Study Questions

1. Who planted the four skinny trees in Esperanza's yard?

2. Does Nenny appreciate the trees?

3. What do the trees say to Esperanza while she sleeps?

4. How is Esperanza like the skinny trees?

5. Why does Esperanza like the skinny trees?

6. What theories do people have about why Mamacita won't come out?

7. How many English words does Mamacita know?

8. What did Esperanza's father eat for three months when he first came to the United States?

9. What does Mamacita's husband want her to do?

10. What does Mamacita's baby learn from the TV?

Answers

1. The city planted the four skinny trees.

2. No, Nenny doesn't even hear them.

3. The trees tell Esperanza to "keep."

4. The trees have skinny necks and pointy elbows, and, like her, they don't belong on Mango Street.

5. She likes the trees because they understand her and give her strength.

6. They guess she won't come out because she is too fat, because there are too many stairs, or because she can't speak English.

7. Mamacita knows eight words in English: "He not here," "No speak English," and "Holy smokes."

8. Esperanza's father ate "hamandeggs."

9. Mamacita's husband wants her to learn English.

10. The baby learns a Pepsi jingle.

Suggested Essay Topics

1. Discuss Esperanza's relationship with the four skinny trees. Why are they so important to her? How do they serve as role models for her?

2. Discuss Mamacita's predicament. Why won't she learn English? Do you think she should?

Part XI: Rafaela Who Drinks Coconut & Papaya Juice on Tuesdays and Sally

New Characters:

Rafaela: *a neighbor of Esperanza*

Rafaela's husband: *locks up Rafaela in the apartment*

Sally: *a friend and classmate of Esperanza*

Sally's father: *who beats Sally*

Cheryl: *Sally's ex-best friend*

Summary

Rafaela Who Drinks Coconut & Papaya Juice on Tuesdays

Rafaela's husband locks her in their apartment on Tuesday nights when he goes to play dominoes. He is afraid she'll run off because she is very young and beautiful. She leans out of the window and watches Esperanza and her friends play, then throws them

money and asks them to buy her juice at the store. She pulls the juice up to her window with a clothesline. Rafaela would like to get out and go dancing at the bar on the corner, where the women are offered sweet drinks and promises.

Sally

Sally, a classmate of Esperanza, is beautiful and admired by the boys. Esperanza also admires Sally, who wears make-up, black clothes, and nylons to school. Sally's father, who is very strict, doesn't let her go out because she is beautiful and he is afraid she will get into trouble.

Sally has no friends after she fights with Cheryl, who called her a name. The boys tell stories about Sally, but Esperanza says those stories are lies. Esperanza wonders what Sally thinks about when she stands alone in the schoolyard and why Sally always has to go straight home. She wonders if Sally sometimes wants to leave Mango Street and find a house where no one will watch her, where no one will criticize her for wanting to love.

Analysis

Young, beautiful Rafaela becomes a prisoner because she is so beautiful. Her husband is afraid that Rafaela, who is "too beautiful to look at," will be tempted by others who will try to woo her away from him. He treats her more like a pet than a person, locking her inside when he goes out. He doesn't trust her or respect her. Instead, he treats her like a piece of property that he must lock up to protect from thieves.

Rafaela asks Esperanza and her friends to buy her sweet juices, hoping that the sweetness will counteract the bitterness of her situation. She envies the women in the corner bar, women who can dance and who have their own keys to their own homes. These women, however, are not really to be envied. Though they are always being offered "sweeter drinks" and always getting promises "to keep them on a silver string"—the men are always promising them better and better things—when the women marry, they often end up locked inside like Rafaela.

Sally, too, is very beautiful, and she is also punished for it. Though Esperanza has lamented her own lack of beauty, she seems to be better off than the women who are beautiful. Sally's father "says to be this beautiful is trouble," and he is very strict with Sally. He won't let her out of the house after school. His strictness makes her rebel. When she gets to school, she applies make-up, which she removes before she goes home. Her orders not to talk to boys make her want to do it all the more, for what is most forbidden is also usually most desired.

Sally seems to be friendless since her fight with Cheryl. The cause of the fight isn't made entirely clear, but it ends their friendship when Cheryl calls Sally "that name"—presumably, "whore." Everyone, it seems, talks about Sally, but Sally has no one to talk to.

Esperanza offers her friendship to Sally in this vignette. She notices how Sally changes when it's time to leave school and return to the home she "can't come out of." Esperanza senses in Sally a similar desire to go "far away from Mango Street" to a house "where a room is waiting" for her, a house in the open, without people watching her and criticizing her, waiting, as the jealous often do, for her "to make a mistake." Instead, Sally would be allowed to dream and love. Esperanza sees Sally's desire for attention from boys as a desire to be loved, and she doesn't think that is crazy. She sees a bit of herself in Sally, because Sally, like her, "never belonged here anyway." Their dreams are different.

Study Questions

1. Why does Rafaela's husband lock her up on Tuesday nights?
2. Where does Rafaela want to go?
3. What does Rafaela ask the girls to do?
4. What does Rafaela wish for?
5. What does Sally's father say about her beauty?
6. What does Esperanza want to learn from Sally?
7. What does Esperanza's mother say about wearing black?
8. Why aren't Sally and Cheryl friends anymore?
9. What does Sally do before she goes home from school?
10. What do most people seem to think of Sally? What are they waiting for?

Answers

1. Rafaela's husband is afraid she'll run away while he's out playing dominoes.

2. Rafaela wants to go to the bar on the corner so she can dance.

3. Rafaela asks the girls to buy her sweet juice from the store.

4. Rafaela wishes for "sweeter drinks."

5. Sally's father says that being beautiful is dangerous.

6. Esperanza wants Sally to teach her how to put on make-up and paint her eyes "like Cleopatra."

7. Esperanza's mother says wearing black when you're young is dangerous.

8. Sally and Cheryl got in a fight and Cheryl insulted Sally.

9. Sally takes off her make-up before she goes home.

10. Most people think that because Sally is beautiful, she is bad. They are waiting for her to get into trouble.

Suggested Essay Topics

1. Discuss Rafaela's situation. Why does she get locked inside? Why doesn't she do anything about it?

2. Esperanza seems to admire and understand Sally. What does Esperanza admire? Why? What does she see in Sally that the others don't?

Part XII: Minerva Writes Poems and Bums in the Attic

New Characters:

Minerva: *a neighbor and friend of Esperanza*

Minerva's husband: *frequently beats his wife*

Summary

Minerva Writes Poems

Minerva, who is just a few years older than Esperanza, already has two children. She also has a husband who beats her. Minerva often kicks her husband out, but he apologizes and she lets him come back, only to have him beat her again. Minerva cries often, and at night, when she is alone, she writes poems on scraps of paper. She and Esperanza share their poems with each other.

Bums in the Attic

Esperanza wants a house like the ones her father takes the family to see on Sundays—a house on a hill with a garden. Esperanza refuses to go with them anymore because she's ashamed of the way they stare hungrily at the houses. She declares that one day she'll have her own house and won't forget where she came from. She'll take in bums who pass by and let them sleep in the attic, because she knows how it feels not to have a home.

Analysis

Minerva, whose "luck is unlucky," is caught in a cycle. Her husband beats her, and she kicks him out. When he apologizes, she lets him return—and he beats her again. He is the husband "who left and keeps leaving"—but she lets him keep returning, probably because she is very young (just "a little bit older" than Esperanza) and has two children to take care of. If she is strong enough to break the cycle with her husband, however, she will end up in another cycle, raising her children alone, just like her mother did.

The vignette, therefore, is filled with images of circles. Minerva cries night and day, around the clock; the kids eat round pancakes for dinner; and the paper on which Minerva writes her poems "smell like a dime."

Minverva asks Esperanza an important question: "What can she do?" This is a difficult question. Neither of Minerva's prospects—kicking her husband out for good and struggling with her children on her own or simply sustaining her husband's abuse—are appealing. Esperanza's "answer" is "There is nothing I can do." She understands that only Minerva has the power to help herself. She is in the cycle; she must break it.

There is, however, something Esperanza can do, and is doing: sharing poems with Minerva. In Esperanza, Minerva knows she has a companion with whom she can share her thoughts, with whom she can express herself. This is probably more important to Minerva than either of them realize, and it may be the one thing that keeps Minerva going. If Minerva keeps writing, it may set her free. Despite Minerva's constant sadness, there is hope that she will break the cycle.

In "Bums in the Attic," Esperanza breaks a cycle she has been caught up in. Until now she has been trying to forget who she is and where she came from. Now, she says, when she gets her own house, she "won't forget." She has realized that people "who live on hills...forget those of us who live too much on earth." Either they never knew what it was like to "live too much on earth" (to be without a real home), or they have tried to forget that they didn't always live on hills; and so their houses are closed to those who are without. Esperanza wants the contentment of the hill dwellers, but not their indifference. Her happiness will come not from forgetting, but from remembering and from helping those without a home.

It is significant that Esperanza doesn't go to see the houses anymore. Her family is offended, but they don't understand that she is ashamed of "all of us staring out the window like the hungry" and that she is "tired of looking at what we can't have." They continue to dream and talk of winning the lottery, but Esperanza is tired of waiting for their someday to come. Now she is thinking about her own someday.

Study Questions

1. How old is Minerva?

2. What does Minerva do "every night and every day"?

3. What do Esperanza and Minerva share?

4. What is Minerva's biggest trouble?

5. Is there anything Esperanza can do to help Minerva?

6. Where does Esperanza's father work? What does he do?

7. Why doesn't Esperanza want to go with the family to look at the houses anymore?

8. What does Esperanza think about people who live on hills?

9. What will guests in Esperanza's house think is causing the noise in her attic?

10. What does Esperanza say she'll never forget?

Answers

1. Minerva is just a little older than Esperanza, probably no more than 18.

2. Minerva cries and prays.

3. Minerva and Esperanza share their poems.

4. Minerva's biggest trouble is her husband, who beats her and "keeps leaving."

5. Esperanza says that there's nothing she can do.

6. Esperanza's father is a gardener who works in the gardens of the houses on the hill.

7. Esperanza doesn't want to go because she is ashamed.

8. Esperanza thinks the people on the hills are so close to the stars that they don't have the worries of people who live "too close to the earth," like trash and rats.

9. Her guests will ask if rats are making the noise.

10. Esperanza says she'll never forget who she is and where she came from.

Suggested Essay Topics

1. Minerva is another woman who is "trapped." She is not physically trapped like Sally or Rafaela; rather, she is trapped in a cycle. Discuss her predicament.

2. How does Esperanza's decision to let bums into her house show a change in her since the beginning of the novel? What is she beginning to realize?

Part XIII: Beautiful & Cruel, A Smart Cookie, and What Sally Said

New Characters:

Izaura and Yolanda: *friends of Esperanza's mother*

Summary

Beautiful & Cruel

Esperanza says she is the ugly girl in the family, so no husband will come for her. Nenny, who is pretty, says she won't wait around forever for a husband. She wants to be able to choose who or what takes her away from home. Esperanza says that Nenny can talk about choices because she is pretty. Esperanza decides not to "grow up tame" and grow old waiting for a husband. She wants to be powerful like the beautiful women in the movies, so she decides to get her power from a different source: she begins to behave like a man.

A Smart Cookie

Esperanza's mother says that she "could've been somebody"— a singer, perhaps, or an artist—but she isn't because she quit school. She confesses to Esperanza that she quit because she was ashamed of her clothes.

What Sally Said

Sally's father has been beating her. She tells people at school that she fell, but no one believes that's how she got her bruises. She says her father never hits her hard, but Esperanza knows that more than once he has lost control and beaten Sally very badly. He beats her because he doesn't want her to bring shame on the family like his sisters did.

Once Sally tried to stay with Esperanza's family for a while, but Sally's father came to get her. He said he was sorry for what he'd done and that it wouldn't happen again. A few days later, however, when he saw her talking to a boy, he beat her so badly she couldn't come to school for several days.

Analysis

Esperanza believes that beauty is a form of power: it allows women like Nenny, who "has pretty eyes," to "pick and choose." Esperanza isn't beautiful, but she wants to be like the women in the movies: the "beautiful and cruel" women who are independent and powerful because their beauty gives them control of men. Esperanza decides to rebel against the patriarchal society that expects her to suppress her individuality and "grow up tame." She decides she won't be "like the others who lay their necks on the threshold waiting for the ball and chain." This is a powerful image—waiting for marriage is like waiting for the guillotine, and marriage is a form of slavery. Given the marriages Esperanza sees around her, however, it should not be a surprise that this is how she views marriage.

To fight against the powerful force of *machismo*, Esperanza decides to wage a "quiet war." She will not fill the traditional female role. Instead, she will behave like a man, leaving her dishes at the table instead of clearing them away. She is beginning to act like her independent, wild great-grandmother, and that should give us hope. Esperanza lives in a different world where a woman cannot simply be thrown over the shoulder like a sack and forced to marry. She is much more likely to win her war.

That is, if she doesn't let shame stop her. In "A Smart Cookie," we learn that shame—which Esperanza has felt so acutely in a number of vignettes—prevented Esperanza's mother from being "somebody." Her mother, who is a first generation Mexican-American, has many talents—she can sing, draw, and speak two languages fluently—but she has no diploma, and, hence, no independence. Though she has lived in their city all her life, she can't go on the train downtown without Esperanza's help. She has built herself a small, "safe" world in the Chicano community and in her home, but she longs to see the world outside it.

Esperanza's mother is adamant that Esperanza finish school and do well. She wants Esperanza to have what she did not—an education and a career, something more to live for than just a man. Women who live only for their men are "fools," she says, citing Madame Butterfly, who kills herself because the man she loves leaves her. She also mentions two of her friends, Izaura and

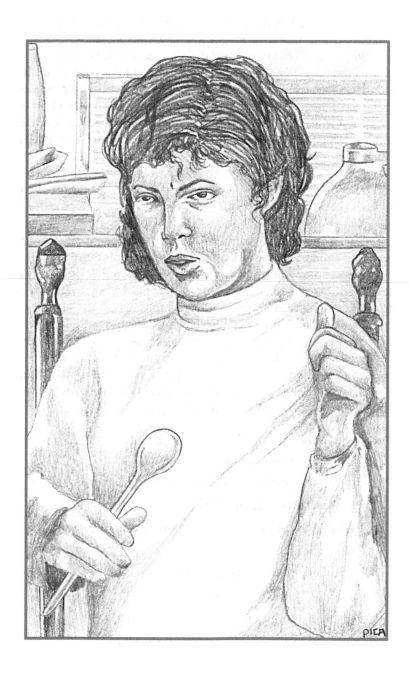

Yolanda, who are lost without their husbands. "Got to take care all your own," her mother says (got to be independent).

What made Esperanza's mother quit school was shame. She was ashamed of her clothes, which weren't "nice." This brings to mind "Chanclas," where Esperanza almost "quit" because she was ashamed of her shoes. Older and wiser, Esperanza's mother is now disgusted with herself. She realizes that her lack of education has left her trapped, like so many others, behind the same rolling pin Alicia is trying to avoid.

Shame is a very powerful emotion, as Esperanza knows. She must learn to avoid it, to be happy with herself no matter what clothes she wears or where she lives, because shame does indeed "keep you down."

It is shame, too, that drives Sally's father to beat her as if she were "an animal." His sisters brought shame on his family by running away—they ran off with men or because of men—so Sally's father refuses to let her wear make-up or talk to boys. When she tries to escape to Esperanza's house he tells her it's the last time, but his shame runs too deep. As soon as he saw Sally "talking to a boy...he just went crazy, he just forgot he was her father between the buckle and the belt." Because he is the one with power, his shame keeps Sally down as well, trapped inside the house after school and perpetually black and blue. Sally's potential to be "beautiful and cruel" is literally being beaten out of her.

Study Questions

1. What has Esperanza decided she will not do?

2. Why does Esperanza begin a "war"? What does she have?

3. How will she fight this war?

4. What kinds of things can Esperanza's mom do?

5. What can't she do?

6. What would Esperanza's mother like to do someday?

7. Why did Esperanza's mother quit school?

8. What advice does Esperanza's mother give her?

9. How does Sally explain her bruises at school?

10. Why does Sally's father beat her?

Answers

1. Esperanza has decided she will not be "tame."

2. Esperanza begins a war because she is not beautiful.

3. She will fight this war by behaving like a man instead of a woman.

4. Esperanza's mother can speak two languages, sing opera, and fix TVs.

5. Esperanza's mother can't take a train by herself into town.

6. Esperanza's mother would like to go to a play and see a ballet.

7. She quit school because she didn't have nice clothes, and she was ashamed.

8. Her mother tells her to stay in school and study hard, because shame will keep her down.

9. Sally says her bruises came from falling.

10. Her father beats her because he is afraid she will bring shame on the family.

Suggested Essay Topics

1. What is Esperanza's "quiet war" all about? Who or what is her enemy in this war? Why?

2. Discuss the danger of shame. What did it do to Mrs. Cordero? What affect did it have on her life? What affect might it have on Esperanza's?

3. Why does Sally's father beat her? Discuss how he handles his fears?

Part XIV: The Monkey Garden, Red Clowns, and Linoleum Roses

New Characters:

Tito's mother: *who Esperanza runs to for help*

Man at carnival: *a man who molests Esperanza*

Sally's husband: *a salesman*

Summary

The Monkey Garden

Esperanza describes the monkey garden, a neighborhood garden where the previous owners kept a pet monkey. The garden has since grown wild and is now a place where they can play and disappear for a while. Esperanza describes the last time she went there, the time she wanted to die.

Esperanza wanted to play in the garden with the other children, but someone said she was too big to play. She urged Sally to join her, but Sally wanted to stay with Tito and his friends. Sally flirted with the boys and they stole her keys. To get them back, they said, Sally had to give them each a kiss. Sally agreed.

This infuriated Esperanza. She ran to Tito's mother and told her what was happening, hoping Tito's mother would stop them. Tito's mother, however, was unconcerned. When Esperanza tried to "save" Sally herself, Sally and the boys told her to go away. Esperanza hid herself in the garden and cried. She wished her heart would stop beating. When she left the garden, it no longer seemed like a good place to her.

Red Clowns

Esperanza says Sally lied to her about what it is like to be with a man. Esperanza had been waiting for Sally at the carnival while Sally went off with a boy. Esperanza waited for a long time, but Sally never came back. Then a man grabbed Esperanza and she couldn't get away from him. He kissed and touched her and told her he loved her. Esperanza tried to make him stop, but he wouldn't. She says everything Sally and all the others had told her about love was a lie.

Linoleum Roses

Sally marries a marshmallow salesman. She tells Esperanza she married him because she's in love, but Esperanza thinks she married him "to escape." Sally says she's happy—she has a lot of nice things now—but her husband sometimes loses his temper and he won't let her talk to or see her friends. He won't even let her look out the window. All she can do is look at the things inside.

Analysis

The monkey garden used to be a sanctuary for Esperanza, but in this long, descriptive vignette, it becomes a symbol of her childhood and innocence, something that Esperanza must leave behind.

The garden had been a place of freedom, a place where they could hide from each other and their mothers, where things could be hidden "for a thousand years." But Esperanza cannot hide from the fact that Sally has crossed a line that Esperanza does not want to cross. Esperanza is still being pulled by the garden, a place Sally won't go anymore because her stockings might get muddy. But Esperanza still wants to run with the others; she doesn't listen to whoever it is that tells her she is "getting too old to play the games." To Sally, those who play in the garden are kids—and she is not a kid anymore.

The distance between Sally and Esperanza here is wide. Sally has "her own game" now, a game Esperanza doesn't understand. She is angry when Sally decides to play Tito's game because it indicates Sally's readiness to move on and become a woman, something Esperanza is not ready to do. It seems natural enough to Tito's mother, but then, she is the mother of a boy. Had it been Sally's mother Esperanza had gone to, the mother's reaction would have been quite different. There is a suggestion of a double standard here, where boys are free to explore their sexuality but girls are not.

Esperanza's attempt to save Sally makes her look ridiculous to Sally and the boys, and she feels ashamed. Hidden in the garden, she tries to will her heart to stop—but it won't. When she gets up, her feet, which were so significant in two other vignettes that deal with Esperanza's developing awareness of her sexuality ("Chanclas" and "The Family of Little Feet"), don't "seem to be [hers] anymore. And the garden that had been such a good place to play didn't seem [hers] either."

This is the last time Esperanza goes to the garden. She leaves it feeling as if it had rejected her wish to die. But in reality, a part of her did die there—her childhood. She leaves the garden, having crossed the line she must cross in order to be accepted by her peers. It is time for Esperanza to stop playing in the garden. Esperanza is not ready to be initiated into "womanhood," but in "Red Clowns," she is literally forced into it. Esperanza had been angry at Sally for playing with the boys instead of in the garden, partly because she was afraid that Sally would abandon her for boys. And that's precisely what happens at the carnival. Sally runs off with a boy and leaves Esperanza waiting alone. Before Sally's tryst is over, Esperanza is raped, her innocence wrenched away from her.

This vignette is an indictment of a society that glorifies sex, making young ones like Sally yearn for a man's touch while leaving them unaware of the dark, aggressive side of male sexuality that is suggested much earlier in "The Family of Little Feet" and in "The Monkey Garden," where Sally must offer her body to get her keys back. No one has warned Esperanza of the brutal power of male sexuality, to control and destroy her own sexual development. In this act Esperanza not only loses her virginity, she also loses part of her identity and independence.

Significantly, the man who rapes Esperanza says "I love you," but what he does to her shows not love for Esperanza but self-love. The man who rapes her cares only about his own satisfaction and absolutely nothing about Esperanza. He seems to think that his desire for Esperanza's body is love, but it is merely violence. This desire, however, is what Sally and others have mistaken for love. This is the lie they have told Esperanza.

It is clear that Sally doesn't know what love is. She claims to be in love with the marshmallow salesman, but it's easy to see that she married him, as Esperanza says, "to escape"—to escape her father, his beatings, his prison of a home, and his shame; to escape the eyes of all those waiting for her to get into trouble. But Sally leaves her father's house only to find herself in another jail. She has a house, and pillowcases, and plates, but they are no comfort to her when her husband loses his temper, when she can't talk on the phone, when she can't even look out the window. From her

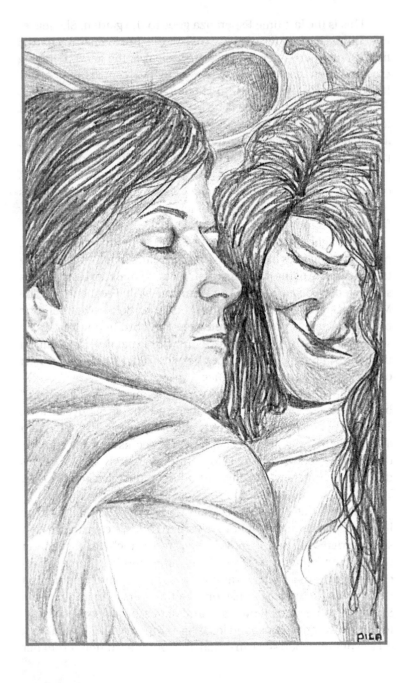

father's house to her husband's, she is transferred from one jail cell to another—another place where she is "afraid to go outside."

Esperanza says Sally likes to look at the walls, at "how neatly their corners meet," and at the roses on her shiny linoleum floor. Her house may be beautiful and neat, but it is still a jail.

Study Questions

1. What happened in the garden after the monkey left?
2. Why did they go to the garden?
3. What does Sally have to do to get her keys back?
4. What does Esperanza do to try to help Sally?
5. Why does Esperanza want to die?
6. Why does Sally leave Esperanza alone at the carnival?
7. What happens to Esperanza while she is waiting for Sally?
8. What are the lies Esperanza accuses Sally of telling?
9. Why does Sally get married?
10. Why isn't Sally happy?

Answers

1. After the monkey left, the garden grew wild.
2. They went to the garden to play and to "disappear" from their mothers.
3. Sally has to give each boy a kiss.
4. Esperanza tells Tito's mother about their game and then comes to Sally's aid with sticks and a brick.
5. Esperanza wants to die because she doesn't understand Sally's game and because Sally tells her to go away.
6. Sally goes off with a boy.
7. Esperanza is raped.
8. Esperanza says Sally lied about what it felt like to be with a man.

9. Sally gets married to escape.

10. Sally isn't happy because her husband won't let her talk to
    or see her friends.

Suggested Essay Topics

1. Discuss Sally's actions in these three vignettes. What do you
    think of how she treats Esperanza? What do you think of her
    decision to marry?

2. Esperanza accuses Sally of lying to her about love and sex.
    Did Sally lie? Who or what is to be blamed for what happened
    to Esperanza?

Part XV: The Three Sisters
and Alicia & I Talking on Edna's Steps

New Characters:

The Three Sisters: *aunts of Rachel and Lucy*

Summary

The Three Sisters

Lucy and Rachel's baby sister dies. Many visitors come to their
house for the viewing, and Esperanza meets Lucy and Rachel's
aunts there. They call Esperanza over and read her palm. They say
that she is special and tell her to make a wish. She does, and they
tell her it will come true. Then one of the sisters takes Esperanza
aside and tells her that when she leaves Mango Street, she must
remember to return, "to come back for the others." She tells
Esperanza not to forget who she is, because she will always be
Esperanza and will always be part of Mango Street.

Alicia & I Talking on Edna's Steps

Esperanza tells Alicia she is sad because she doesn't have a
house. Alicia reminds her that she lives in the house right next door,
but Esperanza says that she doesn't want to belong to Mango Street;
where she lives isn't a real home. Alicia tells Esperanza that whether

she wants to or not, she does belong to Mango Street, and one day she'll return.

Analysis

The *comadres* are fascinating and very important characters. They are old and mysterious, and they do "not seem to be related to anything but the moon." (The moon is a traditional symbol for women.) More importantly, they "had the power and could sense what was what." They know what is going on with Esperanza; they can see her desire to escape Mango Street. They can also see her strength, and they know "she'll go very far."

The three sisters teach Esperanza, who had been so passionate in her desire to leave Mango Street and have a "real" house and to leave her past completely behind her, the ultimate lesson of the novel: that all of Mango Street, all of the characters who populate these stories, all of the people and places Esperanza has known have made her who and what she is. To reject it will keep her from coming back, and, the sister tells her, it is her duty to come back and help others. "A circle, understand?"

Esperanza then realizes that the wish she had made was a selfish one. We don't know for sure what her wish was, but it's fairly safe to assume that she wished for a "real" house, one far away from Mango Street. This is a wish that would keep her from completing the circle.

The circle is an important symbol in this vignette and in the novel as a whole. A circle is endless—it has no beginning and no end; it is complete; it is entirely equal and whole. There is no beginning and no end, but rather a continuous return. The future is always connected to the past.

What Esperanza lamented in the third vignette ("My Name")—that "I am always Esperanza"—is given new meaning by the sisters, who tell her: "You will always be Esperanza." This "permanence" is something Esperanza should embrace, not resist. When we try to deny a part of us or of our past, it becomes a ghost that will always haunt us. That is why Esperanza is so passionate about leaving Mango Street—the more she denies it, the more it gnaws at her and the more she desires to escape it. She must realize that if she completes the circle—if she leaves and comes back—those whom she helps will later be able to do the same for others.

Though the sisters' message was clear, Esperanza hasn't quite understood it all and hasn't completely accepted it when she talks to Alicia. She still laments that she doesn't "have a house"; she still insists that she doesn't belong. Alicia, the only female character strong enough to have gotten out of Mango Street and escape the "ball and chain," already knows what the sisters mean. Alicia has realized that "Like it or not," they "are Mango Street"—and they are destined to return because they are strong enough to make it out.

Study Questions

1. When did Lucy and Rachel's sister die?

2. Who are *las comadres*?

3. What is the significance of the dog crying and the bird flying in the window?

4. What do the sisters say about Esperanza's name?

5. What does Esperanza wish for?

6. How did Esperanza feel about her wish?

7. Where is Alicia from?

8. How long has Esperanza lived on Mango Street?

9. What does Alicia tell Esperanza about Mango Street?

10. What does Esperanza want before she comes back to Mango Street?

Answers

1. She died in August.

2. *Las comadres* are Rachel and Lucy's aunts.

3. The dog and the bird are bad omens that predict the baby's death.

4. The sisters say Esperanza is a "good, good name."

5. Esperanza wishes for a "real" house.

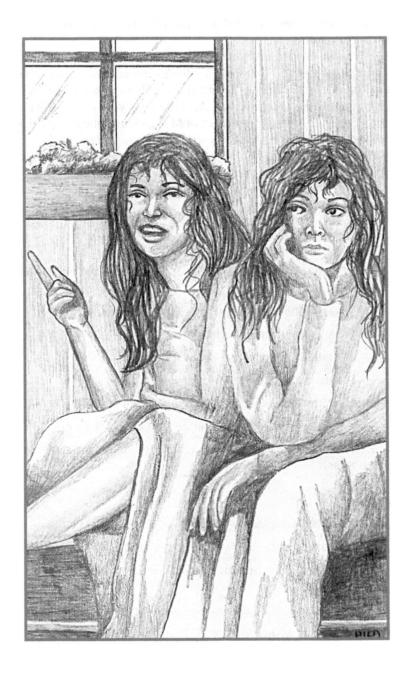

6. She thinks it's a selfish wish.

7. Alicia is from Guadalajara.

8. Esperanza has lived on Mango Street for one year.

9. Alicia tells Esperanza that they belong to Mango Street.

10. Esperanza wants somebody to "make it better."

Suggested Essay Topics

1. Explain the significance of what the aunt says to Esperanza. What does she mean by "a circle"?

2. Both Alicia and the three sisters tell Esperanza the same thing: that she can't deny that she is part of Mango Street, and one day she will return to it. Why? Why can't Esperanza forget where she's from and who she is? Why must she return?

Part XVI: A House of My Own and Mango Says Goodbye Sometimes

Summary

A House of My Own

Esperanza describes the house she wants to have some day: a house completely her own, that belongs entirely to her, with only her things—her books, her stories, her shoes—inside.

Mango Says Goodbye Sometimes

Esperanza says that she likes to tell stories and that she makes up stories about her life as she experiences things. She says she is going to tell the story of a girl "who didn't want to belong." She describes the houses she's lived in and says she remembers the house on Mango Street the most. When she writes this story down, it makes her feel better; it sets her free from Mango Street.

Esperanza says that one day she will leave Mango Street and everyone will wonder where she's gone. They won't know that she left so that she can come back for the others.

Analysis

"A House of My Own" is the shortest vignette in the novel. In it, Esperanza defines the house she longs for. She explains what it is *not* first. It is *not* a house she inherits from a father or inhabits with a husband, and there is "[n]obody to shake a stick at. Nobody's garbage to pick up after." It is not a house where Esperanza will fill the traditional role of homemaker and housekeeper.

Instead, her house will be quiet and clean, a house for her alone, a house made by, and for, herself. It will have only her things: "my porch and my pillow, my pretty purple petunias. My books and stories."

Again, the house is both literal and symbolic. Esperanza is a writer, and artists need their own space to create and to develop their craft. Esperanza wants "a space for myself to go, clean as paper before the poem." Not before a poem, but the poem, the poem to come.

As a woman, Esperanza needs her own space, too—the space to determine who and what she will be, the opportunity to be something other than a daughter and wife. And as a person, she needs to come to terms with, and accept, who she is—her strengths and weaknesses, her fears and her dreams, her uniqueness and her heritage.

This vignette, in its brevity and use of language, is one of the most poetic in the novel. It employs alliteration (porch, pillows, pretty purple petunias) and repetition ("not," "my," and "nobody"), and it is compact—it has the brevity and tight structure of a poem. And, like a poem, it breaks the rules of grammar: every sentence is a fragment. Esperanza breaks these rules to express herself like she will break the "rules" (and roles) that oppress Chicana women.

Before Esperanza begins to write her stories about Mango Street, before she begins to tell the story of the "girl who didn't want to belong," Mango Street has a tight hold on Esperanza because she so desperately wants to get away from it. When she begins to write about it, however, she begins to accept that she is part of Mango Street— "the house I belong but do not belong to." Her writing will slowly enable her to say: I do belong. And this will set her free.

This last vignette explains the structure of the novel. Esperanza, in this final vignette, begins to tell the story of Mango Street. This story begins the same way the novel itself begins, in the exact same words. In the third sentence, however, Esperanza makes an important change. Now what she remembers most is not "moving a lot," but "Mango Street." Writing about Mango Street gives Esperanza courage, courage to realize that she is strong enough to leave Mango Street—and strong enough to come back. She will leave with her papers and books so that she can tell her story.

This story itself is a symbolic return to Mango Street. Esperanza needn't physically come back, though she will. Instead, her words will come to those "who cannot out." By sharing her story, Esperanza will give strength to others.

The novel, then, completes the circle; it is Esperanza's return. It is evidence that she has been freed, and that she has finally found a "real house"—a house within her heart, where she and all the people from Mango Street still reside.

Study Questions

1. What kind of house does Esperanza want?
2. Will anyone live with her in this house?
3. What does Esperanza like to do?
4. Where does Esperanza tell her stories?
5. What story is Esperanza going to tell?
6. What color is the house on Mango Street?
7. What house does Esperanza remember most?
8. What happens when Esperanza writes about Mango Street?
9. What will Esperanza pack when she leaves Mango Street?
10. Why will Esperanza come back to Mango Street?

Answers

1. Esperanza wants a quiet and clean house that's all her own.
2. No, she will live alone.
3. Esperanza likes to tell stories.
4. She tells them to herself, inside her head.
5. She is going to tell her story, the story of Mango Street.

6. Her house is red.

7. She remembers the house on Mango Street the most.

8. When she writes about Mango Street, she feels better and freed from Mango Street.

9. She will pack her books and papers.

10. She will come back to help the ones she "left behind."

Suggested Essay Topics

1. Why does Esperanza insist on a house "all [her] own"? Why can't it be a man's house or a daddy's house?

2. Compare this last vignette to the first. How is it different? Discuss how Esperanza has changed.

3. Discuss the structure of the novel. How is it like a circle? How does the structure of the novel reflect its theme?

Sample Analytical Paper Topics

Topic #1

Discuss the narrative voice and technique of *The House on Mango Street*.

Outline

I. Thesis Statement: *In* The House on Mango Street, *Cisneros employs a unique narrative voice and technique that effectively reflects the theme of the novel.*

II. Esperanza as the narrative voice

    A. Simple vocabulary

    B. Bilingual—use of Spanish terms and code switching (sentences grammatically correct in Spanish but not in English)

    C. Poetic use of language

III. Structure of the novel

    A. Brevity

    B. Fragmentation

    C. Cumulative effect of vignettes

    D. Circular structure

IV. Conclusion

Topic #2

Discuss *The House on Mango Street* as a feminist work of literature.

Outline

I.   Thesis Statement: The House on Mango Street *is a novel that expresses many feminist ideals.*

II.   Feminism

    A.   Definition of feminism

    B.   Feminism vs. *machismo*

III. Women denied equality and independence in *The House on Mango Street*

    A.   Women denied physical freedom

    B.   Women denied sexual equality

    C.   Women denied educational equality

    D.   Women denied opportunity to determine identity and place

IV.   Conclusion

Topic #3

Discuss the symbolism of the house in *The House on Mango Street.*

Outline

I.   Thesis Statement: *In* The House on Mango Street, *the house is the most important symbol.*

II.   A "real" house vs. house on Mango Street

III. House as physical space

IV.   House as a metaphor for the self

    A.   Home in the heart

V.   Conclusion

Glossary of Spanish Terms

Terms found in *The House on Mango Street* and in MAXnotes:

A las Mujeres (dedication)— To the women

abuelito—affectionate term for grandfather (*abuelo*)

Ay, Caray!—Good heavens!

barrios—neighborhoods

bracero—hired hands, temporary immigrant workers

brazer—see *bracero* above

chanclas—old shoes; good for nothing

Chicano—Mexican-American

comadres—female friend, neighbor

cuando—when

El Movimiento and *La Causa*—The Movement or The Cause, referring to the Chicano Movement of the 1960s

Esperanza— hope, expectation

Esta muerto—He is dead.

frijoles—kidney beans

La Revista Chicano-Riquena—The Chicano-Puerto Rican Review los espiritus—the spirits, ghosts

machismo—male chauvinism

Mamacita—little mama

Mamasota—big mama

merengue—meringue; weak person; type of dance

mojado—"wetbacks"—illegal immigrant workers

tembleque—variation of *temblar*, which means to tremble, shake, quiver; by adding "que" to the end, Rachel makes it the name of a dance, like *merengue*

SECTION FIVE

Bibliography

Quotations of *The House on Mango Street* are taken from the following edition:

Ciscernos, Sandra. *The House on Mango Street*. New York: Vantage Books, 1989.

Other Sources:

Ciscernos, Sandra. "Do You Know Me?: I Wrote *The House on Mango Street*." *The Americas Review*. Vol. 15, No. 1, Spring 1987, 77–79.

———. "Ghosts and Voices: Writing from Obsession." *The Americas Review*. Vol. 15, No. 1. Spring 1987, 69–73.

———. "Notes to a Young Writer." *The Americas Review*. Vol. 15, No. 1. Spring 1987, 74–76.

Gomez Quinones, Juan. *Chicano Politics: Reality and Promise 1940–1990*. Albuquerque: University of New Mexico Press, 1990.

Klein, Dianne. "Coming of Age in Novels by Rudolfo Anaya and Sandra Cisneros." *The English Journal*. Vol. 81, No. 5. September 1992, 21–26.

McCracken, Ellen. "Sandra Cisneros' *The House on Mango Street*: Community-Oriented Introspection and the Demystification of Patriarchal Violence." *Breaking Boundaries: Latina Writing and Critical Readings*. Ed. by Asuncion Horno-Delgado, et al. Amherst: University of Massachusetts Press, 1989.

Meier, Matt S., and Feliciano Ribera. *Mexican Americans/American Mexicans: From Conquistadores to Chicanos*. New York: Hill & Wang, 1993.

Novas, Himilce. *Everything You Need to Know about Latino History.* New York: Plume, 1994.

Rodriguez Aranda, Pilar E. "On the Solitary Fate of Being Mexican, Female, Wicked and Thirty-three: An Interview with Writer Sandra Cisneros." *The Americas Review.* Vol. 18, No. 1. Spring 1990. 64-80.

Shorris, Earl. *Latinos: A Biography of the People.* New York: W.W. Norton, 1992.